Collins | English for Exams

GET READY FOR IELTS: READING

PRE-INTERMEDIATE A2+

Els Van Geyte

Collins

Published by Collins
An imprint of HarperCollins Publishers
1 Robroyston Gate
Glasgow
G33 1JN

HarperCollins Publishers
Macken House
39/40 Mayor Street Upper
Dublin 1
D01 C9W8
Ireland

Second edition 2026

10 9 8 7 6 5 4 3 2 1

© HarperCollins Publishers 2012, 2026

ISBN 978-0-00-876543-9

Collins® is a registered trademark of HarperCollins Publishers Limited

collins.co.uk/elt

A catalogue record for this book is available from the British Library

Typeset in by Davidson Pre-Press Ltd

Printed in the UK by Ashford Colour Ltd

All rights reserved. No part of this book may be reproduced, stored in a retrieval system, or transmitted in any form or by any means, electronic, mechanical, photocopying, recording or otherwise, without the prior permission in writing of the Publisher. This book is sold subject to the conditions that it shall not, by way of trade or otherwise, be lent, re-sold, hired out or otherwise circulated without the Publisher's prior consent in any form of binding or cover other than that in which it is published and without a similar condition including this condition being imposed on the subsequent purchaser.

Without limiting the exclusive rights of any author, contributor or the publisher of this publication, any unauthorised use of this publication to train generative artificial intelligence (AI) technologies is expressly prohibited. HarperCollins also exercise their rights under Article 4(3) of the Digital Single Market Directive 2019/790 and expressly reserve this publication from the text and data mining exception.

HarperCollins does not warrant that collins.co.uk/elt or any other website mentioned in this title will be provided uninterrupted, that any website will be error free, that defects will be corrected, or that the website or the server that makes it available are free of viruses or bugs. For full terms and conditions please refer to the site terms provided on the website.

Entered words that we have reason to believe constitute trademarks have been designated as such. However, neither the presence nor absence of such designation should be regarded as affecting the legal status of any trademark.

If you would like to comment on any aspect of this book, please contact us at the given address or online.
E-mail: collins.elt@harpercollins.co.uk

Author: Els Van Geyte
Project lead: James Maroney
Editor: Julie Moore
For the Publisher: Gillian Bowman, Fiona McGlade
Typesetter: Davidson Pre-Press Ltd, UK
Printer: Ashford Colour Ltd, UK

Acknowledgements

We would like to thank those authors and publishers who kindly gave permission for copyright material to be used in the Collins Corpus. We would also like to thank Times Newspapers Ltd for providing valuable data.

Photo credits

All images © Shutterstock.com

About the author

Els Van Geyte worked at the University of Birmingham (UK) for over two decades, as a Principal Educational Developer and as a teacher of English for Academic Purposes. She is also the author of *Reading for IELTS* and of *Writing: Learn to Write Better Academic Essays* (Collins Academic Skills).

MIX
Paper | Supporting responsible forestry
FSC
www.fsc.org
FSC® C011748

Contents

Unit title	Topic	Exam focus	Page
Introduction			4
1 Friendship	Leisure time	Multiple-choice questions	10
2 Body and mind	Health and feelings	Short-answer questions	16
3 Studying abroad	Education	Completing tables and flow charts	22
Review 1			28
4 Science and technology at home	Science and technology	Completing sentences	30
5 Back to nature	The natural world	Completing and labelling diagrams	36
6 Communication	Communication	Completing notes and summaries	42
Review 2			48
7 Business management	Business	Matching information	50
8 Arts and literature	Arts and literature	Matching sentence endings	56
9 Community matters	Society	Matching features	62
Review 3			68
10 Back in time	History	Matching headings	70
11 Crime detection	Crime	Identifying information; True / False / Not given questions	76
12 Travel	Places and travel	Identifying writers' view or claims; Yes / No / Not given questions	82
Review 4			88
Practice test			90
Answer key			100
Glossary			124

Introduction

Who is this book for?
Get Ready for IELTS Reading has been written for learners with a band score of 3 or 4 who want to achieve a higher score. Using this book will help you improve your pre-intermediate reading skills for the IELTS Academic Reading test.

You can use *Get Ready for IELTS Reading*:

- as a self-study course. We recommend that you work systematically through the 12 units in order to benefit from its progressive structure.
- as a supplementary *reading skills* course for IELTS preparation classes. The book provides enough material for approximately 50 hours of classroom activity.

Get Ready for IELTS Reading

- The book contains **12 units**. Each unit focuses on a different topic and these topics are ones that often appear in the IELTS exam.
- After every three units, there is a **Review unit** which helps you to revise the language and skills covered in the previous units.
- At the end of the book the **Practice test** gives you the opportunity to take an IELTS-style test under test conditions.
- There is also a full **Answer key** at the back of the book so you can check your answers. Here you will find suggested answers for more open-ended questions and model answers for the exam practice questions in Part 3 of the unit.
- The **Glossary** at the back of the book lists the useful words from each unit with their Cobuild dictionary definitions.

Unit structure
Each unit starts with the **Aims** of the unit. They outline the key language and skills covered.

Part 1: Language development provides exercises on vocabulary related to the topic as well as any relevant grammar points related to the IELTS Task covered in the unit. Clear structures are provided.

Part 2: Skills development provides information and practice on the task types you will come across in the IELTS Reading test. An explanation of each task type is followed by exercises of increasing difficulty. These exercises give you the opportunity to practise the skills that are needed to complete the task, and they help you to develop strategies for completing these tasks in the test.

Part 3: Exam practice provides realistic exam practice questions for the tasks you have been practising, in a format that follows the actual exam. You can use this to check your progress towards being ready for the test.

Finally, a **checklist** summarises the key points covered in the unit.

Other features
Exam information boxes in each unit provide key background information about the IELTS Reading exam.

Exam tip boxes provide essential exam techniques and strategies.

Watch out! boxes highlight common errors in the exam.

Study tips
- Each unit contains approximately three hours of study material.
- Try to answer the questions without looking at a dictionary to develop the skill of guessing the meaning of unknown words from context. This is important because dictionaries cannot be used during the actual exam.
- Use a pencil to complete the exercises, so that you can erase your first answers and do the exercises again for revision.
- Try to revise what you have learnt in Parts 1 and 2 before doing the practice IELTS questions in Part 3. This will improve the quality of your answers, and using the new language will help you to remember it.
- It's recommended that you try and complete all questions in the unit as the skills needed to do well at the IELTS test can only be improved through extensive practice.
- Read the answer key carefully as this provides information on what kind of answer is correct.
- In Part 3 you are given the opportunity to put the strategies that you have learnt in Part 2 into practice. Remember to read the question carefully and complete the task in the exact way you have been asked. Do not assume that you know a particular task because you have practised similar ones in the past. There may be slight variations in the tasks in the actual IELTS test.

Other resources
Also available in the *Collins Get Ready for IELTS* series are: *Writing*, *Listening* and *Speaking*.

Free Teacher's Notes for all units are available online at: collins.co.uk/eltresources

The International English Language Testing System (IELTS) test

IELTS is jointly managed by the British Council, Cambridge ESOL Examinations and IDP Education, Australia. There are two versions of the test:
- Academic
- General Training

Academic is for students wishing to study at undergraduate or postgraduate levels in an English-medium environment.

General Training is for people who wish to migrate to an English-speaking country. This book is primarily for students taking the Academic version.

The test
There are four modules:

Listening 30 minutes, plus 10 minutes for transferring answers to the answer sheet.
NB: the audio is heard only once.
Approx. 10 questions per section
Section 1: two speakers discuss a social situation
Section 2: one speaker talks about a non-academic topic
Section 3: up to four speakers discuss an educational project
Section 4: one speaker gives a talk of general academic interest

Reading 60 minutes
3 texts, taken from authentic sources, on general, academic topics. They may contain diagrams, charts, etc.
40 questions: may include multiple choice, sentence completion, completing a diagram, graph or chart, choosing headings, yes/no, true/false questions, classification and matching exercises.

Writing Task 1: 20 minutes: description of a table, chart, graph or diagram (150 words minimum)
Task 2: 40 minutes: an essay in response to an argument or problem (250 words minimum)

Speaking 11–14 minutes
A three-part face-to-face oral interview with an examiner. The interview is recorded.
Part 1: introductions and general questions (4–5 mins)
Part 2: individual long turn (3–4 mins) – the candidate is given a task, has one minute to prepare, then talks for 1–2 minutes, with some questions from the examiner.
Part 3: two-way discussion (4–5 mins): the examiner asks further questions on the topic from Part 2, and gives the candidate the opportunity to discuss more abstract issues or ideas.

Timetabling Listening, Reading and Writing must be taken on the same day, and in the order listed above. Speaking can be taken up to 7 days before or after the other modules.

Scoring Each section is given a band score. The average of the four scores produces the Overall Band Score. You do not pass or fail IELTS; you receive a score.

IELTS and the Common European Framework of Reference

The CEFR shows the level of the learner and is used for many English as a Foreign Language examinations. The table below shows the approximate CEFR level and the equivalent IELTS Overall Band Score:

CEFR description	CEFR level	IELTS Band Score
Proficient user	C2	9
(Advanced)	C1	7–8
Independent user	B2	5–6.5
(Intermediate – Upper Intermediate)	B1	4–5

This table contains the general descriptors for the band scores 1–9:

IELTS Band Scores		
9	Expert user	Has fully operational command of the language: appropriate, accurate and fluent with complete understanding.
8	Very good user	Has fully operational command of the language, with only occasional unsystematic inaccuracies and inappropriacies. Misunderstandings may occur in unfamiliar situations. Handles complex detailed argumentation well.
7	Good user	Has operational command of the language, though with occasional inaccuracies, inappropriacies and misunderstandings in some situations. Generally handles complex language well and understands detailed reasoning.
6	Competent user	Has generally effective command of the language despite some inaccuracies, inappropriacies and misunderstandings. Can use and understand fairly complex language, particularly in familiar situations.
5	Modest user	Has partial command of the language, coping with overall meaning in most situations, though is likely to make many mistakes. Should be able to handle basic communication in own field.
4	Limited user	Basic competence is limited to familiar situations. Has frequent problems in understanding and expression. Is not able to use complex language.
3	Extremely limited user	Conveys and understands only general meaning in very familiar situations. Frequent breakdowns in communication occur.
2	Intermittent user	No real communication is possible except for the most basic information using isolated words or short formulae in familiar situations and to meet immediate needs. Has great difficulty understanding spoken and written English.
1	Non user	Essentially has no ability to use the language beyond possibly a few isolated words.
0	Did not attempt the test	No assessable information provided.

Marking

The Listening and Reading papers have 40 items, each worth one mark if correctly answered. Here are some examples of how marks are translated into band scores:

Listening: 16 out of 40 correct answers: band score 5
            23 out of 40 correct answers: band score 6
            30 out of 40 correct answers: band score 7

Reading: 15 out of 40 correct answers: band score 5
            23 out of 40 correct answers: band score 6
            30 out of 40 correct answers: band score 7

Writing and Speaking are marked according to performance descriptors.

Writing: examiners award a band score for each of four areas with equal weighting:
- Task achievement (Task 1)
- Task response (Task 2)
- Coherence and cohesion
- Lexical resource and grammatical range and accuracy

Speaking: examiners award a band score for each of four areas with equal weighting:
- Fluency and coherence
- Lexical resource
- Grammatical range
- Accuracy and pronunciation

For full details of how the examination is scored and marked, go to: www.ielts.org

The IELTS Test: Formats

There are two formats for the IELTS test. One is paper-based, and the other is computer-based. The difference is in the test-taking experience, not in the content. Both test formats have the same questions and marking criteria. The Speaking part of the test is conducted face to face with an examiner for both the paper and computer based tests.

The formats are different as follows:

Delivery

- **Paper-based** – The candidate writes their answers for the Listening, Reading, and Writing sections on physical paper using a pen or pencil.
- **Computer-based** – The candidate types their answers for the Listening, Reading, and Writing sections on a desktop computer.

Test Environment

- **Paper-based** – Tests are held in large rooms with many other candidates.
- **Computer-based** – Tests are conducted in smaller rooms with fewer candidates, and each candidate has their own computer station.

Listening Test

- **Paper-based** – Candidates listen to the audio recording played through speakers in the room. Candidates have 10 minutes at the end of the Listening test to transfer their answers from the question booklet to the answer sheet.
- **Computer-based** – Candidates wear headphones and listen individually. Candidates have 2 minutes at the end of the Listening test to review their answers because the answers are typed directly into the computer as candidates listen.

Reading Test

- **Paper-based** – Candidates read the passages and answer the questions in a physical booklet. Candidates can highlight or underline text with a pen or pencil.
- **Computer-based** – Candidates see the passages and questions side-by-side on a screen and type their answers into the computer. Candidates can use on-screen tools to highlight text and make notes.

Writing Test

- **Paper-based** – Candidates write their essays by hand. Candidates must write clearly. Candidates have to count their words manually.

- **Computer-based** – Candidates type their essays using a keyboard. Candidates can use cut, copy, and paste to edit their texts. The screen provides a live word count.

Results

- **Paper-based** – Results are typically available 13 calendar days after the test date.
- **Computer-based** – Results are available much faster, usually within 1 to 5 days.

Scoring

Each section is given a band score. The average of the four scores produces the Overall Band Score. You do not pass or fail IELTS; you receive a score.

1 Friendship

Language development | Vocabulary related to: leisure time
Exam skills | Working with key words
Exam practice | Answering multiple-choice questions

Part 1: Vocabulary

1   2   3   4

1a What do we need friends for? Match the words to the pictures. The first one has been done for you.

sharing   chatting   having fun   partying

1 _partying_
2 _____
3 _____
4 _____

1b Words ending in *-ing* are often at the beginning and at the end of sentences. Put the four words from exercise 1a in the correct sentences.

1 It is difficult for young children, but they have to learn that friendship is about _____ .
2 _____ with friends is not something I do very often, but we always celebrate our birthdays.
3 _____ with friends is one of my favourite ways to spend an afternoon. We have so much to say that we often talk for hours.
4 Even on bad days, being with my best friend means _____ .

❗ Watch out

Certain nouns go with certain verbs. We often use *play* with activities, games or sports that we play to win and that involve equipment, e.g. *play tennis*. For individual activities, we often use *do*, e.g. *do weightlifting*. For activities ending in –ing, such as *swimming*, we often use *go*. When reading, try to notice verbs and nouns that go together.

Unit 1

2 Which nouns go with which verbs? Identify the correct answer for each of the sentences. Choose from:

        yoga   basketball   board games   dancing

1 When I was younger, I made a lot of friends by playing team sports. For example, twice a week after school I played …

2 I still do a lot of exercise, and I now regularly do online …

3 On a Saturday night, I like to go …

4 In my spare time I also like to meet up with my friends, e.g. last Saturday people came to my house. We ordered pizza and played …

3a Read about how these people have fun. Underline all the words that refer to activities, and circle the words that refer to places. Don't use a dictionary yet.

Jack, 15:
I spend time with my family most evenings. At the weekend, I prefer to hang out with my friends at the park, or in the playground in the local woods. If it rains, I like to go to see a film with my friends.

Monica, 18:
I go to a chess club which meets twice a month, and once a year we go camping. It's the highlight of my summer! We stay in tents on a lovely camp site and have picnics and barbecues. In the evenings, we organize quizzes and play cards. And we also play a lot of chess, of course!

Amrita, 12:
My older sisters spend a lot of time with their friends in the local shopping centre, but I'm not allowed to go out without an adult yet. I still chat to my friends a lot after school though, but I go online to do that.

3b Find words in the texts above that match with these meanings.

1 _____ : a large place where you can buy many different things

2 _____ : a person who is no longer a child

3 _____ : a place where you can stay in a caravan or a tent

4 _____ : a meal in the open air

5 _____ : outdoor parties where people cook and eat food

6 _____ : games in which you have to answer questions

Friendship   11

Part 2: Skills development

Exam information: Multiple-choice questions

In the exam, there are different types of multiple-choice questions: you may be asked to choose the correct answer to a question, or you may be given a choice of sentence endings and asked to form a sentence that reflects the meaning of the text. The questions will be in the same order as the information in the text.

1 Read the following text and then look at the questions on the next page.

The value of friendship

Recent research into the world of teenagers has suggested that they value friendship above everything else. Children aged between 12 and 15 were asked what was important to them. Their answers included possessions such as money and computer gadgets but also relationships with people. The teenagers questioned said that friends were the most important to them, more even than family, or boyfriends and girlfriends.

We wanted to find out more about the results of this research so we asked our readers what they thought about the value of friendship. Here are some examples of what they said about their friends:

Ben, 15:
Every time I have a fight with my parents, I need some time on my own. But after that, the first thing I do is meet up with my friends. After playing football for a while, or skateboarding, I usually feel much happier again.

Rory, 13:
When I moved to the countryside, I thought that it would be the end of my friendships. But my old friends have kept in touch and they come and visit in the holidays. There's a lake nearby, so we often go sailing, water-skiing or windsurfing. And I have made some new friends here too, at school, and since I joined the rugby club.

Carlos, 11:
Last year, I broke my arm on a skiing holiday. Unfortunately, it was my left arm and I am left-handed. My school friends all helped and copied their notes for me.

It seems that our readers value their friendships very highly. From what they told us, they spend a lot of time with their friends, just hanging out, or sharing hobbies and interests. They seem to need their friends for advice, help, chats, and for having fun. Clearly, friends make each other feel better. Looking at what our readers told us, the results of the recent research are not really surprising.

Unit 1

2 Try to answer this question yourself first, before reading the explanation. Choose the best answer from the letters a–d.

To teenagers, money is …

  a not important.
  b as important as computer gadgets.
  c as important as relationships with people.
  d less important than friendships.

The correct answer is d. The teenagers said that money, gadgets and relationships are all important to them. However, the text also tells us that the teenagers value friendships most, therefore money is less important.

Exam tip

Deciding which are the key, or most important, words in a question can help you to locate the appropriate section of the text more quickly.

3 Look at the questions in Exercise 4, without reading the answer options. Underline the question words (e.g. *where, when, what*) and the key words in each of the questions (1–3) and sentence stems (4–5).

4 Now answer these multiple-choice questions. Choose the appropriate letter a, b, c or d.

  1 *Why are Ben, Rory and Carlos mentioned in the article?*
    a They know why teenagers value friendship.
    b They gave information about themselves.
    c They read magazines.
    d They are teenage boys.

  2 *Which of the following best describes Ben?*
    a He often has fights.
    b He likes being alone.
    c He is happier than his friends.
    d He likes some sports.

  3 *What do we know about the lake that Rory visits?*
    a It is near the school.
    b It is near his home.
    c It is used by a lot of people who do water sports.
    d It is in a village.

  4 *Carlos mentions that he is left-handed because …*
    a it makes skiing harder.
    b it makes it worse that he broke the arm he uses most.
    c it is an interesting fact about himself and he was talking about his left arm.
    d it is very unfortunate when you break your left arm.

  5 *The answers to the recent research and the answers from the readers …*
    a were surprising.
    b were the same.
    c were similar.
    d were both about sports.

Part 3: Exam practice

Questions 1–6

Read the text below. Choose the appropriate letters a, b, c or d.

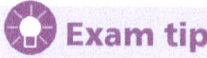
Exam tip
If a question is difficult, don't spend too much time on it – go to the next one. Once you find the next answer, you can go back in the text to find the answer to the previous question. This is because, in this type of task, the questions are in the same order as the information in the text.

1   How many friends do the majority of people probably have at any particular point?
   a   30 or fewer
   b   a minimum of 30
   c   400
   d   150

2   It is difficult …
   a   to believe the numbers about friendship.
   b   to keep your friends happy.
   c   to trust what you read on social media.
   d   to give a definition of 'friendship'.

3   Friendship means …
   a   different things to different people.
   b   dying for your friends if you need to.
   c   helping each other until it is no longer necessary.
   d   accepting people with different views.

4   Sometimes people worry because …
   a   they think that they have too many friends.
   b   they spend too much time with friends.
   c   they think they are too old to make friends.
   d   there are no guidelines about friendship.

5   Many of us …
   a   are dissatisfied with our friends.
   b   build friendships late in life.
   c   are frightened to talk to strangers.
   d   need to be with others.

6   What does 'Strangers are friends we have not met yet' mean?
   a   We have not met strangers before.
   b   Strangers are also our friends.
   c   We should not talk to strangers.
   d   Strangers may become our friends.

It is said that most people have no more than 30 friends at any given time, and 400 over the whole of their lives. However, on social media platforms, most users have 150–180 friends or followers. If these numbers are correct, then friendship means different things in different situations.

One of the reasons for having more online friends than real friends at a certain point in time is that online friendships do not require much time and energy: it is easy to accept friendships and keep them forever. Another possibility is that it is difficult to say 'no' when somebody asks us to be their friend online, even if we feel we don't really know them. The fact that they ask us suggests that they do consider us a friend, which is a nice feeling. Alternatively, they may be 'collectors' of online friends and just want to use us to get a higher number of friends and appear to be popular.

Online friendships are quite easy, but in the real world decisions about friendships are harder to make. There are no rules about friendship. There are no guidelines about how to make friends, how to keep friendships going, and how to finish friendships if we want to move on. People have very different opinions about this: some people would die for their friends and they value them more than family. Others say that friends are temporary, only there to help each other until they are no longer needed. If people with such different views become friends, this can lead to problems.

Because of these different views of friendship, it is easy to be unhappy about our friendships. We may want them to be deeper or closer, or we may want to have more friends in our lives. Sometimes we simply do not have the time to develop our friendships, or we fear we have left it too late in life to start. If we move to another country or city, we have to find ways to make new friends again.

This dissatisfaction shows us how important friendships are for most of us. We should not think that it could be too late to build friendships. We also need to understand that the need to be around other people is one that is shared by many. Therefore, we should not be too frightened about starting to talk to people who in the future may become our friends: it is likely that they too would like to get closer to us. Remember what people say: strangers are friends we have not met yet.

▶ Progress Check: Multiple-choice questions

How many boxes can you tick? You should work towards being able to tick them all.

Did you ...
remember to underline the key words in the questions and look for them in the text? ☐
read only the parts of the text that you needed to? ☐
remember that the questions are in the same order as the information in the text? ☐
first skip a difficult question and then go back to it after you found the answer to the next one? ☐

2 Body and mind

Language development | Vocabulary related to: health and feelings
Exam skills | Keeping to word limits
Exam practice | Short-answer questions

Part 1: Vocabulary

1a These words are related to health. Write the words under the matching pictures.

diet   fitness   age   illness

1 _____   2 _____   3 _____   4 _____

1b Copy the table and write the following words in the right categories.

sport   teenager   disease   injury   nutrition   exercise
youth   vegetables   training   ageing   fruit   medicine
adult   gym   nuts   medical condition

Diet	Fitness	Age	Illness

16 Reading for IELTS

Unit 2

2a The words below describe feelings. Are they positive or negative feelings? Copy and write the words in the right categories. Use a dictionary if necessary.

amazed	angry	annoyed	bored	confident	curious
depressed	disappointed	embarrassed	guilty	jealous	
	nervous	relaxed	tired		

2b Write the adjectives next to their matching nouns. Only look back at the box in 2a if you need help.

amazement
anger
annoyance
boredom
confidence
curiosity
depression
disappointment
embarrassment
guilt
jealousy
nervousness
relaxation
tiredness

2c Underline which of the two words best fits in each sentence.

1 Confidence/Anger is a healthy human emotion, but it can also lead to problems.
2 There is no need for jealousy/embarrassment during an appointment – doctors are there to help with all kinds of medical conditions.
3 Guilt/Boredom can have a bad effect on your health, so it is important to keep busy and active.
4 Depression/Disappointment is a common medical condition.
5 If you have problems sleeping, there are steps you can take to deal with your tiredness/nervousness.
6 Relaxation/Curiosity exercises can improve sleep and general health.
7 To her amazement/annoyance, the medicine worked immediately.

Body and mind

Part 2: Skills development

Exam information: Short-answer questions

In the exam, you may have to look for facts in a passage and give short answers to questions. You will be told how many words you are allowed to use in the answers. A number can be written either as a word, e.g. *four*, or as a number, e.g. *4*, and counts as one word. A word with a hyphen in it, e.g. *mother-in-law*, counts as one word. You will not be required to use contractions. All answers must be taken from words in the text.

1 How many words are there in these sentences?

1 She keeps fit by running after her two five-year-olds.
2 To use the gym equipment safely, follow the step-by-step instructions.
3 The internet is helping the over-sixties to find up-to-date health information.
4 They are offering exercise classes 3 mornings a week for the part-time workers.

Exam tip
Read the instructions carefully and keep to the word limit. If the instruction is that your answer needs to be 'NO MORE THAN ONE WORD AND/OR A NUMBER', you can write one word, one number, or a word and a number.

2 The following instructions were given in an IELTS reading exam: 'Using NO MORE THAN TWO WORDS AND/OR A NUMBER, answer the following questions.' The student answer in the table below is factually correct. Make it shorter *if necessary*.

Questions	Students answers	Correct short answer
1 During which decade was the world health statistics survey carried out?	in the twenty-twenties	
2 Which specific global disease does Chapter 1 discuss?	the COVID-19 pandemic	
3 How does the report highlight what has been done to address health issues?	country-focused stories	
4 How did they manage to collect the data?	global monitoring of e.g. publications	

18 Reading for IELTS

3 Answer these questions in NO MORE THAN THREE WORDS.

1 What do you think is the best way to lose weight? _____
2 How do you feel about football? _____
3 What do you enjoy doing in your free time? _____
4 Why is exercise important? _____

4 Read this list and cross out two activities that would not help you to answer the questions below.

- reading the questions slowly before reading the text
- identifying the key words in the questions
- reading the text before reading the questions
- identifying the key words in the text
- scanning (moving your eyes down over the text to find information you are looking for, without reading every word)

5 Underline the key words in questions 1–3.

1 What does the younger generation usually think health means?
2 To feel healthy, what do older people feel they still need to be able to do?
3 Who could benefit from the results of the survey?

6 Now scan the text below and answer questions 1–3, using NO MORE THAN TWO WORDS from the text for each answer.

1 _____
2 _____
3 _____

Illness is defined in a variety of ways, which depend on a number of factors. One of these factors is age differences. Older people tend to accept as 'normal' a range of pains and physical limitations which younger people would define as symptoms of some illness or disability. As we age, we gradually redefine health and accept greater levels of physical discomfort. In Blaxter's (1990) national survey of health definitions, she found that young people tend to define health in terms of physical fitness, but gradually, as people age, health comes to be defined more in terms of being able to cope with everyday tasks. Her study is a good reminder for health professionals to consider many factors when examining patients, including what patients themselves expect from their health at their age. There are now plans to repeat this survey to find out whether age differences are a similar factor in the definition of health in other countries.

Part 3: Exam practice

> **ⓘ Exam information: Short-answer questions**
> Just as with multiple-choice questions, short-answer questions are normally in the same order as the information in the text.

Questions 1–6

Answer the questions below using NO MORE THAN TWO WORDS from the text below for each answer.

1 According to studies, whose health suffers the most because of social circumstances?
   _____

2 What type of health problem is strongly related to a lack of money?
   _____

3 Which kinds of communities prefer everyone to have small body shapes these days?
   _____

4 In the past, which people were considered rich if they were big?
   _____

5 Give examples of fixed characteristics that people may not like about themselves.
   _____

6 What characteristic are people likely to try to improve?
   _____

Questions 7-8: Multiple choice

Choose the appropriate letter a, b or c.

7 What do sociologists think we should do?
   a consider mainly the biological aspects of our minds and bodies
   b think about more than the health of our body, and also consider the health of our mind
   c consider bodies and minds in their historical and societal contexts too

8 Which of the following is an opinion held by the writer?
   a people being big is a mental health, medical and social issue
   b it is wrong and unhealthy to have a large body shape
   c people unfairly believe that being big is wrong and unhealthy

> **The body**
>
> The concept of 'the body' is closely related to the ideas of 'illness' and 'health'. All of us exist in 'bodies' of different shapes, heights, colours and physical abilities. The main reasons for the differences are genetic, and the fact that people's bodies change as they age. However, a huge range of research indicates that there are social factors too.

Poorer people are more likely to eat 'unhealthy' foods, to smoke cigarettes and to be employed in repetitive, physically difficult work or the opposite: boring, inactive employment. Moreover, their housing conditions and neighbourhoods tend to be worse. All of these factors impact upon the condition of a person's health: the physical shapes of bodies are strongly influenced by social factors.

These social factors are also closely linked to emotional wellbeing. People with low or no incomes are more likely to have mental health problems. It is not clear, however, whether poverty causes mental illness, or whether it is the other way around. For example, certain people with mental health issues may be at risk of becoming homeless, just as a person who is homeless may have an increased risk of illnesses such as depression.

There are other types of social factors too. Bodies are young or old, short or tall, big or small, weak or strong. Whether these judgements matter and whether they are positive or negative depends on the cultural and historical context. The culture – and media – of different societies promote very different valuations of body shapes. What is considered as attractive or ugly, normal or abnormal varies enormously. Currently, for example, rich societies highly value slimness, but historically this was different. In most societies the ideal body shape for a woman was a 'full figure' with a noticeable belly, while in middle-aged men, a large stomach indicated that they were financially successful in life. In many traditional African and Pacific island cultures, for example, a large body shape was a sign of success and a shape to be aimed at.

It is easy for people to feel undervalued because of factors they have no power to change, for example, their age and height. Equally, they can feel pressured into making changes to their appearance when there is a choice, which in extreme cases can lead to obsessions with weight loss and fitness regimes.

Sociologists, then, are suggesting that we should not just view bodies and minds in biological terms, but also in social terms. The physical body and what we seek to do with it change over time and society. This has important implications for medicine and ideas of health. Thus, the idea of people being 'obese' is physically related to large amounts of processed food, together with lack of exercise, and is therefore a medical issue. However, it has also become a mental health issue and social problem as a result of people coming to define this particular body shape as 'wrong' and unhealthy.

Progress Check: Short-answer questions

How many boxes can you tick? You should work towards being able to tick them all.

Did you...
remember that the questions are in the same order as the information in the text? ☐
read the questions slowly before reading the text? ☐
use the key words technique? ☐
read the instructions carefully to know what the word limit was? ☐
count the words in your answers? ☐

3 Studying abroad

Language development | Words related to: education
Exam skills | Scanning
Exam practice | Completing tables and flow charts

Part 1: Vocabulary

1a Match the following school subjects to the definitions

1 numeracy   a the study of events that have happened in the past
2 literacy   b the study of the countries of the world and of such things as the land, seas, climate, towns and population
3 history   c the ability to work with numbers and do calculations (+, −, x, /)
4 geography   d the ability to read and write

1b Without looking back at exercise 1, write the correct school subject below each picture.

1 _____ 2 _____ 3 _____ 4 _____

2 Put the following in order, according to level of education. Rank them from low to high.

nursery school   master's degree   PhD
secondary school   bachelor's degree   primary school

6 _____
5 _____
4 _____
3 _____
2 _____
1 _____

3 What do you know about these student destinations and places of origin? Fill in the gaps in the table with words from the list:

Egyptian   Arabic   Brussels   Dutch (x2)   German (x2)   Hanoi
Heidelberg   Japan   Cairo   Kyoto   Maastricht   Vietnam   Zurich

Country	Main languages	Adjective	City with one or more universities
(1) _____	Vietnamese	Vietnamese	(2) _____ Ho Chi Minh City
(3) _____	Japanese	Japanese	Tokyo (4) _____
Egypt	(5) _____	(6) _____	Alexandria (7) _____
Germany	(8) _____	German	(9) _____ Munich
The Netherlands	(10) _____	Dutch	Amsterdam (11) _____
Belgium	(12) _____ French	Belgian	Louvain (13) _____
Switzerland	French, Italian (14) _____	Swiss	Geneva (15) _____

4 In this text from a student newspaper, you will find nouns relating to countries in brackets. Write down the adjectives to complete the text.

To find out why students decided to study abroad, and what their experiences have been, we have been speaking to international students. This week we introduce Alex from Canada, who studies in Belgium.

Alex says: I came to Belgium because of its central location in Europe, the quality of the education and because it is not too expensive to study here. There are three official languages in Belgium, but these do not include **(1)** [England] _____, which is what I speak at home. Luckily, it is the language used for most of the teaching on my course, and it has also been useful that I know **(2)** [France] _____ .

The university has many international students, and I am really pleased that I have already made **(3)** [Vietnam] _____, **(4)** [Japan] _____ and **(5)** [Switzerland] _____ friends. I am hoping to visit their countries one day and invite them to Canada.

It only takes a few hours by train to travel to other countries; I have already visited **(6)** [Germany] _____ and **(7)** [the Netherlands] _____ cities. Belgium itself is also great of course: there is so much history and culture here, and I enjoy the **(8)** [Belgium] _____ food, such as chips, waffles and chocolate.

Part 2: Skills development

ⓘ Exam information: Completing tables and flow charts

In the exam, you may be given a summary with gaps in it, in the form of notes, one or more paragraphs, a table or a flow chart (a series of steps linked by arrows). You will also need to read a text or a particular part of that text to find the missing information, which will probably not be in the same order as the gaps. You will be told how many words from the passage you should use, e.g. *no more than two words and/or a number, one word only*.

- Task type 1: select words from the text to complete the gaps
- Task type 2: choose from a list of words (identified by A,B,C, etc., or drag and drop online)

💡 Exam tip

Scanning is a very useful technique, because it saves time. It means that you move your eyes down the text quickly to find specific information, e.g. places, names, phrases, without reading everything properly and ignoring information you do not need.

The following four exercises help you practise scanning. They all refer to the text opposite.

1. Use the organization of the text to help you. Look at the text quickly to decide which paragraph(s) you would need to read properly if you only wanted to find out about the reasons why people choose to study abroad.

   Paragraph number(s): _____

   ## 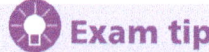 Exam tip
   Use the text style or formatting to help you find the areas in the text that you are looking for, e.g. uppercase letters, numbers, italics, bold print, quotation marks and other visual information.

2. Scan the text to find names of countries, people and organizations. Copy and complete the table.

Countries	People	Institutions or departments

3. Do this exercise in less than one minute if you can. First copy the table in your notebook. Then scan the text for the different items. Check in the Answer key to see if you found them all within the time limit.

numbers	
words in italics	
words in bold print	
abbreviations	

Reading for IELTS

4 Scan the text quickly to answer the following questions.

1 Which paragraph(s) give(s) an individual's opinion?
2 What does Russell really want people to understand?
3 Which two paragraphs talk about the country that is the most welcoming to overseas students?
4 Which paragraph gives examples to explain what an internationalization approach is?

5 How did you find the answers without reading properly?

Is it better to go abroad to study?

Student-friendly places

A recent survey has named the universities that are most welcoming to overseas students. As you would expect, English-speaking countries such as Australia, the UK and the US have made the top 10, but the number one may be a surprise: Germany. Two Far Eastern countries, i.e. China and Malaysia, made it to the top 5, ranking higher than the US, Japan, Russia, Nigeria and Brazil.

The benefits of studying abroad

Russell Howe, a Scot who is currently studying a business degree at Stellinga International College in the Netherlands, previously also studied in India (which came 11th on the list). 'People often ask me why I needed to travel, because British universities have a good reputation elsewhere in the world. But this is not something I *needed* to do, but something I really *wanted* to do. I have learnt different ways of looking at things, but I also found out how much we all have in common, wherever we are from. All of this will be useful in my future career.'

Russell is not the only international student in his department. Business and administrative courses are the most popular with international students, followed by engineering and technology, social studies, creative arts and design, medicine-related topics and law. Manal, a student at the Faculty of Art and Design at Stellinga, says she has similar reasons to Russell, but there is more: 'I wanted to broaden my understanding of the world. I have enhanced my language skills: I am more fluent in English and have also taken a level 1 Dutch evening class. One of my modules is about European art, and I believe that I am benefiting more from studying this in Europe than anywhere else.'

Enabling student access

What is it that makes these countries student-friendly? Well, all of them make it easy for international students to apply, and provide ongoing support once they are there. They also offer good quality degrees, which are valued highly in other countries too. The fact that Germany came out as winner is probably due to the country's efforts towards *internationalization*. One aspect of this is that the country welcomes foreign students by charging them the same fees as home students, meaning that in some universities overseas students study for free. Many classes are in English, and so is most information, making it easier for international students to keep informed and take part in student life.

Part 3: Exam practice

Questions 1–5

Using NO MORE THAN TWO WORDS from the passage below for each answer, complete the table below.

The required documents:

Evidence of language ability	IELTS 6.5 or (1) _____
Evidence of studies	(2) _____, Dutch VWO diploma, or other secondary school diploma
Information about motivation	(3) _____ with a maximum length of (4) _____
Proof of identity	(5) _____ and passport photo

Questions 6–9

Read the passage below. Complete the flowchart using the list of words, A–G, below. Choose the correct letter, A–G.

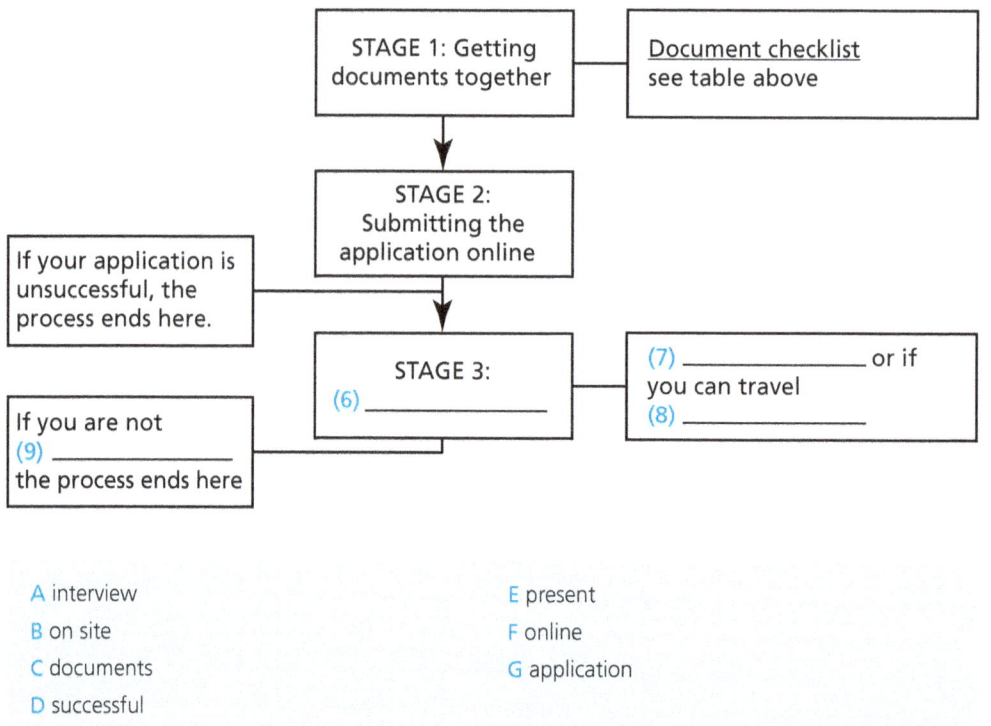

A interview
B on site
C documents
D successful

E present
F online
G application

Applying to Stellinga College

Why Stellinga?
Thank you for your interest in Stellinga International College. As an international student, we are sure you will find our university college an exciting place to study, with like-minded and ambitious individuals.

Preparing and submitting your application
We have tried to make the application process as easy as possible for you, but there are a number of procedures you must follow.

All our courses are taught in English, so first of all you will probably need to submit proof of your English language ability. We require an IELTS score of 6.5 or another test result which is equivalent (see appendix). You will also have to send us your secondary school diploma, so that we can evaluate it. If you have the International Baccalaureate or a Dutch VWO diploma, you don't need to provide English language test results.

We will also require a personal statement. This is a text of up to 1000 words in which you introduce yourself, explain your interest in our college, and why you want to study your chosen course.

If you are from outside the European Union (EU), it is important that you have an entrance visa before you come to study in the Netherlands, but we will apply for this for you.

We now only accept online applications, so please ensure that you have all your documents ready to upload before you begin. Any documents that are not in English originally will also need to be translated and the translations also uploaded.

You will need a passport photograph; a copy of your passport; copies of all your certificates, diplomas, etc.; your proof of language ability (see above); and your personal statement in English.

What happens next?
Your application will then be considered. If your initial application is successful, you will be invited for an interview. This will be conducted online in English or on site, depending on whether you can come and visit us. You will talk to two or three members of staff for up to 30 minutes, and will be asked to elaborate on your application documents and your personal statement. We aim to inform you of our decision in writing, within 4 weeks. There are several possible outcomes: you may not have been successful; you may be offered a place at the college or you may be offered a place on the waiting list. You will need to reply to any offers within two weeks, otherwise your place may be offered to somebody else.
Good luck with your application.

Progress Check: Completing tables and flow charts

How many boxes can you tick? You should work towards being able to tick them all.

Did you …
- use scanning techniques? ☐
- read thoroughly only the parts of the text that you needed to? ☐
- read the instructions carefully to know what the word limit was? ☐
- count the words in your answers? ☐
- only use words that were in the text? ☐

Review 1

1 Answer the following questions about yourself in NO MORE THAN THREE WORDS. This may be difficult to do but it will help you practise keeping within word limits.

   1 What is your favourite meal?
   2 What did you do yesterday?
   3 What is the best thing that has happened to you in your life so far?
   4 What is the best advice you have ever been given?
   5 If you could do anything you wanted right now, what would it be?
   6 What do you dream about?

2 Match the sentence stems with the correct endings. You will not use all of the endings.

   1 I don't mind spending
   2 If you don't like meat, you probably won't like
   3 I have bought
   4 I live near
   5 I like hanging out with my friends
   6 Every Monday there is
   7 I believe that
   8 I like to play

   a a camp site but I never go there.
   b a picnic with my parents in a tent.
   c a quiz at the social club, which is open to anyone.
   d at the shopping centre.
   e that children under 14 should not be left on their own.
   f money is more important than friendship.
   g tennis at the weekends.
   h the piano from a friend.
   i the woods in my spare time.
   j time with my parents, but not when I am on holiday.
   k barbecues.
   l with my friends after college.

3 Match the verbs in the box to the words below to make correct collocations.

   keep   play   study   value   take   charge   have

   1 _____ fees
   2 _____ a class
   3 _____ in touch
   4 _____ fun
   5 _____ friendship
   6 _____ cards
   7 _____ abroad

4 Correct the mistakes, if any, in the following sentences.

1 When I have no college work, I usually go to my friends to play.
2 Party with friends is my favourite activity.
3 There is no need to be embarrassed, just come in.
4 To my amazed, she had prepared a picnic.
5 Depressed is a common medical condition.
6 His worst disease was a broken arm.
7 He plays a lot of yoga.
8 I have been feeling very tiredness.

5 How might these people be feeling?

1 _____ 2 _____ 3 _____

4 _____ 5 _____

6 The following words are related to the topic of education, but all the vowels have been left out. Can you put them back in?

1 ltrc _____
2 nmrc _____
3 stdnt _____
4 nvrsty _____
5 dgr _____
6 rsrch _____
7 dplm _____
8 pplctn _____

4 Science and technology at home

Language development | Vocabulary related to: science and technology
Exam skills | Working with paraphrasing
Exam practice | Completing sentences

Part 1: Vocabulary

 1
 2
 3
 4

1a Match the words to the items.

gas   liquid   solid

1 _____states of matter_____   3 _____
2 _____   4 _____

1b Use the words and phrases from exercise 1a to complete the gaps.

The three **(1)** _____ are solid, liquid and gas. They differ because their particles, the very small pieces they are made from, move in different ways. They can be found all around us.

A **(2)** _____ has a fixed volume and takes the shape of the container it is in, such as a bottle, because its particles are close together but can move. Examples in the home are water and milk.

A **(3)** _____ has a fixed shape and volume because its particles are close together and shake with small, repeated movements. Examples in the home are cupboards and vegetables.

A **(4)** _____ has no fixed shape or volume and can expand to fill its container because its particles are far apart and move rapidly. Examples are nitrogen and oxygen, which we breathe in.

2a Use the information in the table to complete the matching exercise underneath. The first one has been done for you.

Unit 4

Word part	Meaning
-meter	measure, record
-logy	the science or study of something
-graphy	the study of or writing about something
bio-	life
auto-	self
thermo-	temperature
eco-	related to natural surroundings
zoo-	animal
ge(o)-	the earth or land
hydro-	water
chrono-	time

1 barometer
2 chronometer
3 thermometer
4 ecology
5 biology
6 geology
7 zoology
8 hydrology
9 geography
10 hydrography

a an extremely accurate clock that is used especially by sailors at sea
b the study of the relationships between plants, animals, people and their environment, and the balances between these relationships
c the study of the Earth's structure, surface and origin
d the study of the countries of the world and of such things as the land, seas, climate, towns and population
e the scientific study of animals
f the science related to the study of living things
g an instrument that measures air pressure and shows when the weather is changing
h an instrument for measuring temperature, usually consisting of a narrow glass tube containing a thin column of a liquid which rises and falls as the temperature rises and falls
i the study and recording (mapping) of the oceans, seas and rivers
j the study of the distribution, conservation, use, etc. of the water of the Earth and its atmosphere

2b Use the above information to complete the definitions for the following words.

1 *a biography*: _____ about another person's _____
2 *an autobiography*: a book _____

> **Watch out**
>
> Knowing the meaning of word parts can often help you work out the overall meaning, but there are words where this does not work. For example, *dis-* often means 'opposite', *advantage / disadvantage*; *agree / disagree*; *appear / disappear*; *connect / disconnect*; *honest / dishonest*, but sometimes *dis* is not a separate word part or does not have that meaning, as in *disaster, discuss*.

Science and technology at home

Part 2: Skills development

Exam information: Completing sentences
In the exam, you may be asked to complete sentences with words from the passage. The information will be in the same order as the questions.

Exam tip
The sentences will refer to information in the text, but this will be paraphrased and will include synonyms (words or expressions that mean the same) and antonyms (words or expressions that mean the opposite). You should scan the text to look for paraphrases of the sentences to find the section and information you need.

Example:
In the passage you read:
*One property of the new **substance** is that it can be used at **extremely** low temperatures.*
The sentence you need to complete is:
The new **material** is suitable for use at **incredibly** _____ .
The correct answer is:
The new material is suitable for use at incredibly low temperatures.

You were able to complete the sentence by recognizing the synonyms: substance – material; extremely – incredibly

1 Match the words with their (near) synonyms. Use your dictionary when you need to.

1	device	a	investigation
2	research	b	from a distance
3	remotely	c	the future
4	tomorrow	d	gadget
5	substance	e	curiosity
6	interest	f	material

Example:
In the passage you read:
*Most people believe that the original leak was probably **not deliberate**.*
The sentence you need to complete is:
It is generally thought that it was an **accidental** _____ .
The correct answer is:
*It is generally thought that it was an **accidental** leak.*
You were able to complete the sentence by recognising the antonyms: deliberate – accidental

Unit 4

2 Match the words with their (near) antonyms. Use your dictionary when you need to.

1 digital	a the future
2 yesterday	b deliberate
3 remote	c remembered
4 forgotten	d analogue
5 lost	e nearby
6 accidental	f found

3 In the following sentences, underline any words that refer to a similar idea or thing. The first one has been done for you.

1 Your mobile phone contains small amounts of <u>gold and platinum</u>, as well as less <u>valuable metals</u>.
2 There are some materials that allow electricity to pass through them. These electrical conductors are used in many different appliances in the home.
3 Another example is electrical insulators, substances that do not let electricity pass through.
4 Your smartphone's operating system may have the same or a different OS to the one controlling your tablet.

4 Scan the text below for (near) synonyms of the following words. Try to find them all, or as many as you can, in less than 90 seconds. They are in the same order.

1 parts	4 a very large amount	7 transfer
2 typical	5 exceptional	8 following
3 include	6 tiny	9 material

> ### 💡 Exam tip
> Timing is very important in the IELTS exam, as you will have to answer 40 questions about three reading passages in one hour. In this type of exam question, you will be looking for detailed information, so you will need to use your scanning skills. Try to get used to scanning and working as fast as you can.

Mobile phone components
An average basic mobile phone contains a circuit board, an antenna, a liquid crystal display, a keyboard, a microphone, a speaker and a battery.

Mobile metals
Mobiles contain different metals:

- Copper is used for electrical circuits because it is a good electrical conductor.
- Silver is used in switches on the circuit boards and in the phone buttons because it is an even better electrical conductor. It lasts for millions of on/off cycles.
- Gold is used to plate the surfaces of the circuit board and the connectors. It is an excellent electrical conductor and does not corrode.
- Tantalum is used in the electronic components. It enables scientists to make mobiles very small.

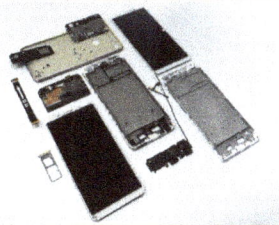

Your mobile is also likely to contain palladium, platinum, aluminium and iron.

Electrical conductivity
Metals conduct electrical currents well. Non-metals usually make good insulators. In a mobile, electrical insulators surround the circuit.

Smart mobiles
The next generation of mobile could be made from 'smart' fabric. These types of fabric react to something in the environment and change. A smart fabric mobile could be folded and put in your pocket without breaking.

Science and technology at home

Part 3: Exam practice

Questions 1–4

Complete the sentences below. Choose NO MORE THAN TWO WORDS OR NUMBERS from the text for each answer.

Exam tip

In the exam, try not to use any previous knowledge you may have on a particular topic. You must always answer according to the information given in the text.

1 A compound cannot be separated without energy and a _____ .
2 Although mixtures consist of a combination of elements and compounds, it is possible for these to be _____ .
3 If flavourings were not added, people would probably _____ to consume margarine.
4 Flavours can only be described as natural if they have a natural _____ .

Questions 5–7

Using NO MORE THAN THREE WORDS for each, answer the following questions.

5 What are artificial flavours? _____ .
6 Why might certain natural flavours be bad for our health? _____ .
7 What flavours should we probably use if we care about the environment? _____ .

Cupcakes are made from a mixture of ingredients. Different flavoured cupcakes have different mixtures. The icing used to decorate the cakes contains sugar, water, colouring and flavouring. Water and sugar are different types of compounds. These compounds are made from elements.

Elements, compounds and mixtures

Chemical substances occur in three types.

- Elements – these contain one type of atom only. They cannot be chemically broken down into simpler substances.
- Compounds – these contain two or more different elements bonded together. A chemical reaction is needed to break up a compound. This will involve energy.
- Mixtures – these may contain two or more elements and/or compounds. They are mixed in any proportion and can be separated out.

When a baker mixes the flour, sugar, fat, eggs, flavouring and colour together to make cupcakes, he or she is making a mixture. The icing sugar, water and colour make a different mixture. The sugar and water are compounds.

The compound water is made from the elements hydrogen and oxygen. Sugar contains the elements hydrogen, oxygen and carbon.

In this unit, we will be looking at flavourings, the substances that are added to food or drink to give it a particular taste. They are added because people would probably refuse to eat certain products without them. Margarine and ice cream, for example, would have unacceptable tastes, whereas certain jellies, some other sweets, and meat replacement products would have little or no taste.

Natural flavours are those found in nature. Those from vegetable sources include vanilla, strawberry, lemon and nuts. An example of an animal source is beef flavouring, added for example to fries. Essential oils and fruit juices can also be used to flavour foods. They are sourced in nature and obtained through physical processes such as distillation and fermentation.

Some animal flavours, such as bacon and beef flavour in snacks, are vegetarian because they are artificial rather than made from animal sources.

There are also nature-identical flavourings. An example is vanillin, which is often produced cheaply from lignin, a polymer, rather than from vanilla pods. These flavourings are chemically identical to natural flavourings, but have been produced chemically rather than naturally, e.g. by a process of chemical extraction. The human body does not notice the difference as their molecules are identical to natural ones.

Artificial flavourings consist of chemically synthesized compounds which have no source whatsoever in nature. Although the word natural typically has positive connotations, some natural flavours may come from contaminated sources, which are harmful. Artificial flavours undergo strict testing because they are subject to laws (e.g. The European Flavouring Regulation (1334/2008) and may therefore be purer and safer. Using natural flavourings is also more expensive and may be considered a waste at a time when we are trying to preserve nature.

Glossary
polymer: a naturally occurring or synthetic compound

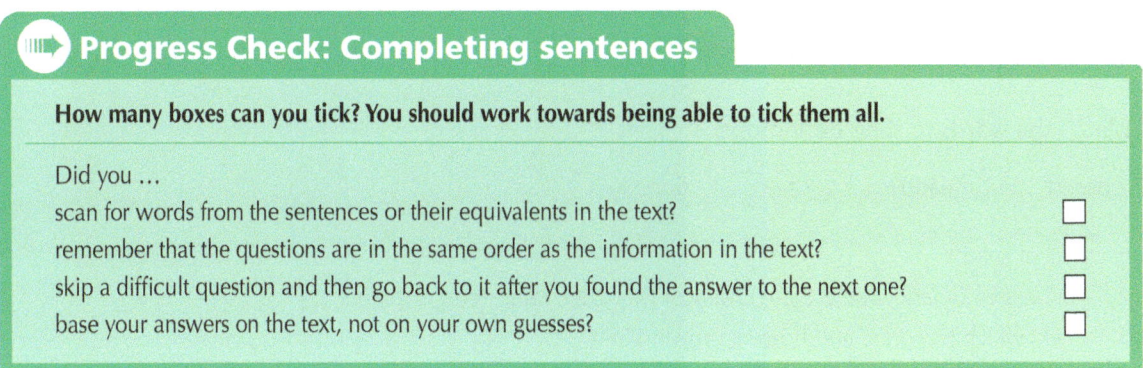

Progress Check: Completing sentences

How many boxes can you tick? You should work towards being able to tick them all.

Did you …
scan for words from the sentences or their equivalents in the text? ☐
remember that the questions are in the same order as the information in the text? ☐
skip a difficult question and then go back to it after you found the answer to the next one? ☐
base your answers on the text, not on your own guesses? ☐

5 Back to nature

Language development | Vocabulary related to: the natural world
Exam skills | Linking words; Skim-reading
Exam practice | Completing and labelling diagrams

Part 1: Vocabulary

1 _____   2 _____   3 _____   4 _____

1 The following words refer to the natural world. Use the words to label the pictures above.

bay   valley   cliff   waterfall

2 Match the words to their definitions.

desert   meadow   cave   dune

1 a hill of sand
2 a large area of land where there is almost no water, rain, trees, or plants
3 a field which has grass and flowers growing in it
4 a large hole in the side of a cliff or hill, or one that is under the ground

3a Read the following texts, without using a dictionary. Underline all the words that refer to the natural world.

Our knowledge of natural history would not be what it is today without the work of women explorers, artists and scientists. In this leaflet, you will learn about three British pioneering women, first to be involved in uncovering some of the rich history of the natural world.

Mary Anning (1799–1847)
Mary came from a poor family who lived in Lyme Regis, a coastal town in the South West of England. Her father tried to make extra money by selling fossils (remains in rocks) to rich tourists. Consequently, Mary and her siblings learned from an early age how to

look for fossils, although she was the only one of the brothers and sisters who became an expert because she understood that fossils were of interest to geology and biology, not just tourism. However, in her lifetime she did not always get the credit she deserved, as it was male geologists who published the descriptions of any finds. Her important finds include the first skeleton of an ichthyosaur, or fish-lizard, a plesiosaur, also known as sea-dragon, and a pterodactyl, a 'flying dragon'.

Collecting fossils on the cliffs was dangerous work. Mary's dog Tray was killed when rocks and earth fell down a cliff, and she nearly lost her life in the same landslide, but in the end it was cancer that killed her when she was 47.

Dorothea Bate (1878–1951)
Born in the Welsh countryside, she had a passion for outdoor pursuits and natural history from an early age. She became the first female scientist in the Natural History museum in London. She was a palaeontologist, that is, a scientist who studies fossils in order to understand the history of life on earth. She went to mountains and cliffs in the Mediterranean and explored hilltops in Bethlehem, discovering and documenting animal fossils. She wrote hundreds of reports, reviews and papers.

Evelyn Cheesman (1881–1969)
Although Evelyn wanted to become a veterinary surgeon, this was not possible for women in the early 20th century. Instead, she trained as a canine nurse. Her first job, however, was not related to dogs: she worked in the insect house at the London Zoological society. She was very adventurous and went on many expeditions to remote locations, as far away as the Galapagos Islands. Despite being very busy, she managed to publish 16 books.

3b Difficult words are often explained in texts. Find the explanations of the following words in the texts. The first one has been done for you.

pioneering: first to be involved in

| pioneering | Lyme Regis | fossils | siblings | ichthyosaur | plesiosaur |
| pterodactyl | Tray | landslide | palaeontologist | canine | remote |

4a Circle or highlight all the linking words (words that show a connection between clauses or sentences) in the text in 3a above.

Exam tip
Linking words can help you follow a text and understand the connection between the point that the writer makes. Notice them and use them to guide you.

4b Use the linking words to help you match the sentence parts. Some are used to connect reasons, other to express contrast.

1 **As** we want bees to visit our garden,
2 We like bees to visit our garden, **but**
3 The pyramids are located in the desert. **However,**
4 The area is known for its hot weather. **Consequently,**
5 **Despite** the great work done by women scientists,
6 People's lives these days are easier **because**

a the children are a little scared of them.
b tourists are advised to use sunscreen.
c history has often forgotten about them.
d we have made it into a meadow.
e so much scientific progress has been made.
f it does occasionally rain there.

Part 2: Skills development

ℹ Exam information: Completing diagram labels

In the exam, you may be asked to read a passage and use words from it to complete labels on a diagram or picture. The answers will often come from a particular section of the text and may not be in the same order as the questions.

1 Skim-reading means reading quickly to find information. Skim-read the passage below and tick when you have found the sections that refer to:

what jellyfish look like ☐	how fossils are formed ☐
what barnacles are ☐	how seashells are formed ☐

Part one: **The beach, a natural treasure trove**

Nature walks can be fun, energizing and educational at the same time. In Part One, we will look at what we can find on a marine walk. In Part Two, we will discuss our fascinating forests.

First of all, when you are walking on the beach you may be able to spot tracks. Birds and crabs leave footprints behind, especially in wet sand. On sandy beaches you will also be able to find interesting holes, made by crabs that were digging for food in the mud.

You may also come across jellyfish, as these are often washed up on the beach by the tides. They have no eyes, ears, heart or head and are mostly made of water. They look like a bag with arms, which are called tentacles. These contain poison, which helps them catch food. Even when they are out of the water or in pieces the tentacles may sting you, so they are best left alone.

Other animals you may find are coral and barnacles. The latter are marine animals that are related to crabs and lobsters and live in shallow waters. They like to attach themselves to hard materials, so you are likely to find them stuck to a piece of wood.

You may also see what look like small gelatinous blobs but are actually fish or worm eggs.

If you are lucky, you may find a fossil. In essence, this is an animal that died and got buried in a sea bed. They are likely to look like a piece of rock with an imprint of an animal skeleton. Their history is very interesting.

For an animal to become fossilized, it has to be buried in mud, sand or soil. If an animal dies but is not buried, it is more likely to rot away, be swept away by wind or water, and/or be eaten by another animal. Over millions of years, the animal remains become buried deeper and deeper; the mud, sand or soil compresses and slowly becomes rock. Their bone or shell starts to crystallize, because of surrounding minerals and chemicals. Ideally, the temperature stays relatively constant throughout this long process. Sometimes the fossil dissolves completely and just leaves an imprint. At other times, waves, tides and currents slowly make the rocks erode, which allows the animal remains to break off, ready for you to find.

What you will definitely find on a beach are shells. These were once the homes of animals such as snails, barnacles and mussels, consisting of a hard layer that the animal created for protection as part of its body. After the animal has died, its soft parts have rotted or have been eaten by other animals, such as crabs. What is left is a beautiful seashell for you to admire.

Unit 5

2 Cover the diagrams below. Now try to make your own drawing(s) to represent the information in the paragraph about how fossils are formed.

3 Using **NO MORE THAN FOUR WORDS** from the passage, complete each gap in the diagram.

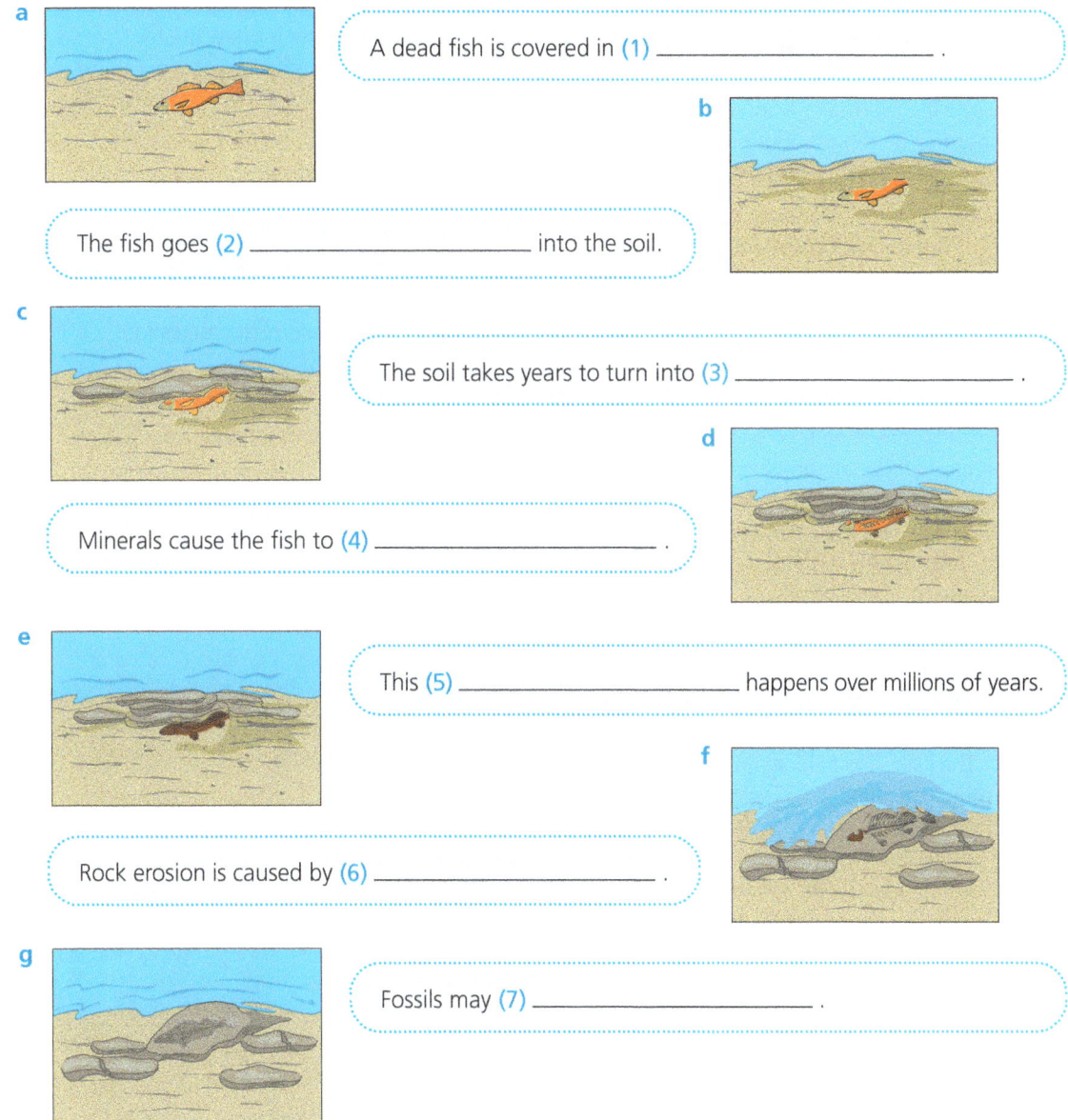

a A dead fish is covered in (1) _____ .

b

The fish goes (2) _____ into the soil.

c

The soil takes years to turn into (3) _____ .

d

Minerals cause the fish to (4) _____ .

e

This (5) _____ happens over millions of years.

f

Rock erosion is caused by (6) _____ .

g

Fossils may (7) _____ .

Back to nature 39

Part 3: Exam practice

Using NO MORE THAN TWO WORDS from the passage, complete each gap in the diagram.

The many uses of the Moringa tree

The Moringa tree, Saragwa, or Drumstick tree, is relatively unknown in the West, despite the fact that it is incredibly useful. Miriam Tayne reports about its culinary, medicinal and other uses.

The Moringa tree is a relatively small tree that typically grows to between three and ten metres tall. Its flowers are creamy-coloured and have been compared to small orchids. The plant has long and round green pods that can grow to 30 cms and which look a bit like drumsticks, hence the tree's common name. The pods consist of three parts, which contain round, dark brown seeds. Planting needs to be done in sandy or muddy soil, using these seeds or tree cuttings. The plant does not tolerate frost but thrives in hot climates. It is very common in South and South-east Asia, Africa and America.

The leaves are reputed to have anti-inflammatory and anti-bacterial properties, so are used for eye and ear infections, fevers, etc. They are also held against the forehead to reduce headaches, or made into tea to treat stomach complaints. As they contain a lot of iron they have been used for the treatment of anaemia, a medical condition in which there are too few red cells in the blood, causing tiredness. The plant also contains many other nutrients, such as phosphorus, calcium, potassium, and vitamins A and C.

The ground-up seeds are commonly used to treat certain skin infections, but can be used for much more. Ground seeds can be mixed with salt or oils to apply to the body to treat cramp, back ache and forms of arthritis, a medical condition in which the joints are swollen and painful. The oil, called Ben oil because it contains behenic acid, is also used as a hair treatment or a perfume, and to deter mosquitoes and treat their bites. The by-products of the oil manufacturing process are used for fertilization and water purification.

The roots work in exactly the same way as the seeds, but are much stronger, so are not used as often. They have additional uses for heart and circulation problems, whereas the gum is sometimes used to treat asthma. The bark has quite a pleasant taste and is sometimes eaten to encourage digestion.

The plant's main use is as food: for livestock, and for human beings, because it contains high concentrations of fibre and protein. The drumsticks are eaten in soup and/or as green beans, often in combination with shrimp (see picture), whereas the seeds are eaten like peas, or roasted. The leaves are eaten fresh or cooked in similar ways to spinach. Chopped, they are used as a garnish on soups and salads. They are often pickled or dried so that they are always available to use in sauces, stir-fries, soups and in sweet and sour or spicy curries.

Like every other part of the tree, its flowers are not just decorative but also functional. They taste a bit like wild mushrooms and are considered a delicacy. They are used to make tea to treat the common cold, mixed with honey to make cough medicine, and made into juice to be drunk during breastfeeding as it is said to increase milk flow.

There is not a part of the tree that is not used. The Moringa tree is probably the most beneficial tree in the world.

Unit 5

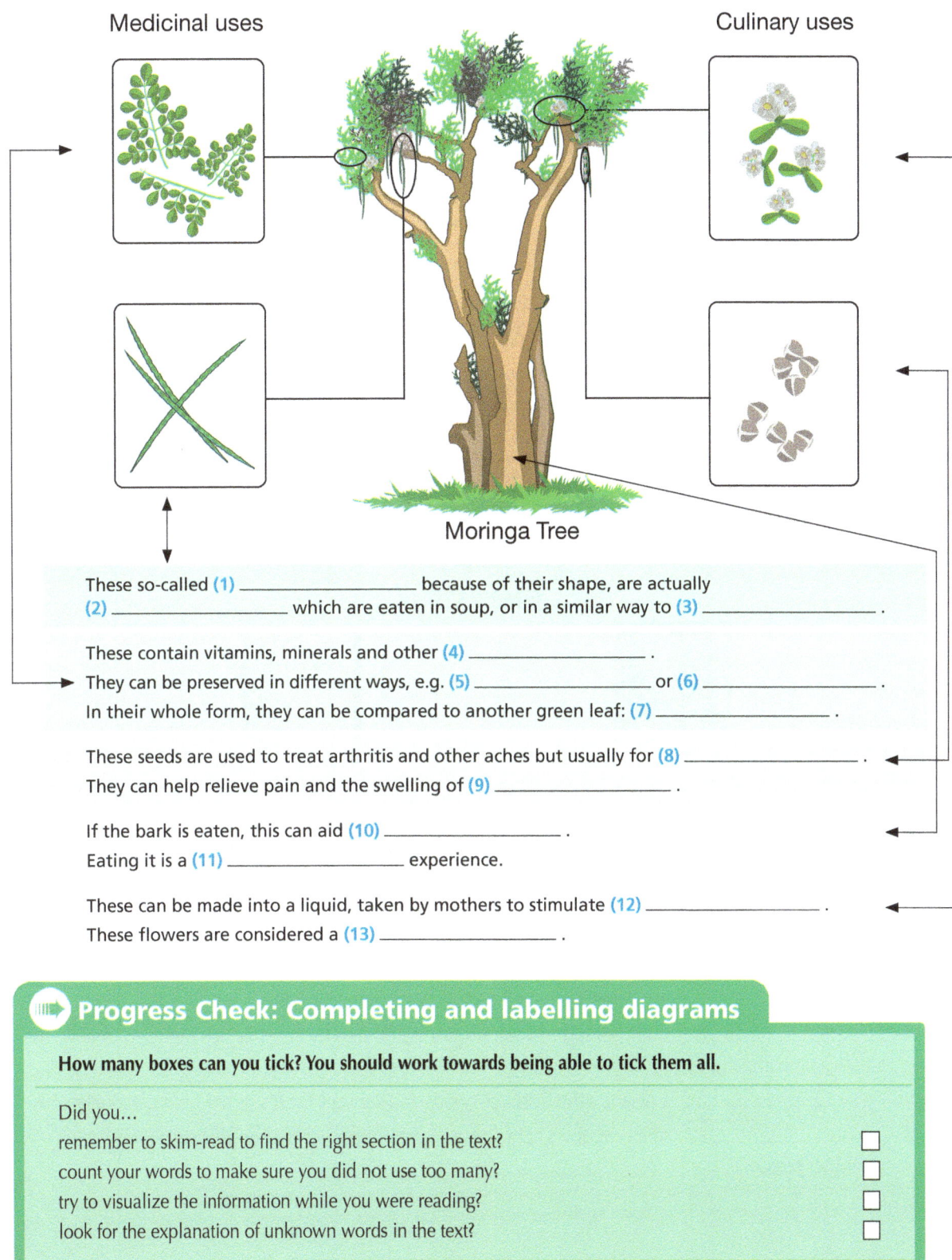

These so-called (1) _____ because of their shape, are actually (2) _____ which are eaten in soup, or in a similar way to (3) _____ .

These contain vitamins, minerals and other (4) _____ .
They can be preserved in different ways, e.g. (5) _____ or (6) _____ .
In their whole form, they can be compared to another green leaf: (7) _____ .

These seeds are used to treat arthritis and other aches but usually for (8) _____ .
They can help relieve pain and the swelling of (9) _____ .

If the bark is eaten, this can aid (10) _____ .
Eating it is a (11) _____ experience.

These can be made into a liquid, taken by mothers to stimulate (12) _____ .
These flowers are considered a (13) _____ .

Progress Check: Completing and labelling diagrams

How many boxes can you tick? You should work towards being able to tick them all.

Did you…
remember to skim-read to find the right section in the text?   ☐
count your words to make sure you did not use too many?   ☐
try to visualize the information while you were reading?   ☐
look for the explanation of unknown words in the text?   ☐

Back to nature

6 Communication

Language development | Vocabulary related to: communication
Exam skills | Predicting answers
Exam practice | Completing notes and summaries

Part 1: Vocabulary

1 When starting a company, you need to find ways of letting people know about it. What types of communication has this restaurant used? Label the pictures with the words in the box.

slogan   advertisement   logo   sign

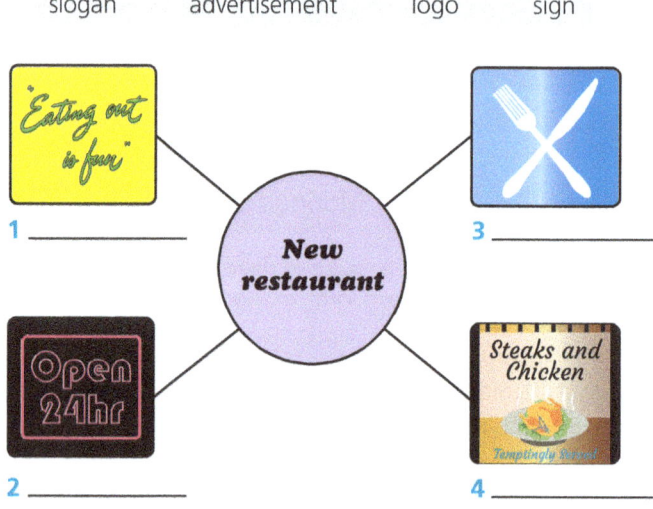

1 _____
2 _____
3 _____
4 _____

2a In the opposite text, underline the words that refer to types of communication. Don't use a dictionary. Then find words that mean:

1 _____: unwanted emails sent to a large number of people, as a way of advertising

2 _____: the practice of a company paying for its product to be placed in a clear position in a film or television programme as a form of advertising

3 _____: very large signs on which posters are displayed

4 _____: small printed notices, usually distributed by hand, which are used to advertise a particular company, service or event

5 _____: a person who acquires goods and services for his or her own personal needs

6 _____: small windows containing an advertisement that appear on a computer screen

It's impossible to avoid advertisements. In our homes, newspaper, magazine, television and online ads compete for our attention. Posters, billboards and flyers greet us the moment we walk out the door. Advertising agencies stay busy thinking up new ways to get our attention. We have company logos on our clothes. Our email is full of spam, and pop-ups slow us down when we read articles on our social media feeds. Product placements sneak into films and TV shows. On free streaming channels we are unable to skip the TV commercials. Advertisers have also tried advertising in a subliminal way (influencing viewers' minds without them knowing it), e.g. by using colour, shapes or sounds in ads to strengthen brand awareness. It's no wonder that this is called the consumer age.

2b Find words in the above text that collocate (go together with) the words in the table.

1	*newspaper*		6		logos
2			7		placements
3		ads	8		commercials
4			9		awareness
5		agencies	10		age

3 Complete the passage with the words in the box.

brands   consumers   opinions   audience   trust   products

Social media influencers are people who have a large (1) _____ of followers on online platforms such as TikTok, which allows them to influence the (2) _____ and behaviours of these followers. Businesses and (3) _____ often sponsor influencers to promote their (4) _____ and services, as (5) _____ increasingly place their (6) _____ in personal recommendations.

> ⚠️ **Watch out**
>
> Articles are small words that can contain a lot of information. Look at these slogans:
>
> *Go to work on an egg.* (The Egg Council)
> *The ultimate driving machine.* (BMW)
>
> The first slogan, which uses the indefinite article (*a/an*) suggests that any egg will do. The second one uses the definite article (*the*) to suggest that there is only one ultimate driving machine, a car from their specific brand.

4 Do the following nouns relate to general or more specific information? Complete the sentences with *a(n)* or *the*.

1 _____ brand or business can really benefit from working with an influencer.
2 Within seconds of leaving your house, you will probably see _____ advertisement.
3 I quite enjoy watching _____ TV commercial for the first time.
4 Technology is very important in _____ world of advertising.
5 Yellow is _____ colour to be seen in this season.

Part 2: Skills development

Exam information: Completing notes and summaries

In the IELTS exam, you may be given a summary of, or notes about, a text, but there will be information missing which you will have to look for. You will usually find the information in a particular part of the text, but not in the same order. You will either have to choose words from the text or choose the correct option from those given.

1 Copy and complete the table. Some words belong in more than one category.

Exam tip
It is often easier to choose the correct answer if you can predict the type of word you need by using your knowledge of grammar.

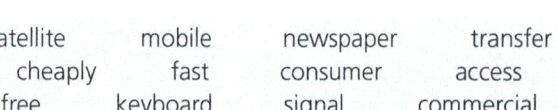

nouns	verbs	adverbs

2 Read the sentences. Predict what type of word is missing in each gap and give an example of a possible answer. The first one has been done for you.

1 Websites allow us to _____ a library's catalogue of books and periodicals.
   a verb; e.g. see, view, access

2 Public libraries are becoming more digital, but you can still borrow and _____ books, magazines and other media.

3 *Communication* refers to both the act of _____, in other words the exchange of information, ideas or feelings, and something that is _____, for example an email or text.

4 The advertising industry keeps coming up with new ideas. For example they now work a lot with influencers as this can be a _____ way to reach a specific audience than TV commercials.

5 Sign language is a visual way of communicating that uses body language. It is _____ used by Deaf people and those with hearing loss, but is also _____ used by others, e.g. to help children develop language skills.

6 After 1066, many French and Latin words came _____ the English language.

3 Here are some notes (a) and a summary (b) based on the text below.

- Use your skim-reading and/or scanning skills to find out which sections of the text they come from.
- Then use your knowledge of grammar to identify the missing words.

Use no more than TWO words from the text in each gap.

a
```
types of communication:
(1) _____
(2) written       } verbal
(3) _____
```

b

It is important to follow the rules when communicating in writing, especially if you are in a (1) _____ environment. There are three areas which are important: (2) _____, content and language. The language needs to be formal and there should be no (3) _____ . You cannot choose to include exactly what you like, for example financial information must be included in your yearly business (4) _____ .

In all communication, whether this is verbal or non-verbal, a sender transfers a message to a receiver, choosing a certain medium. The receiver uses the message clues and the context, and decodes it to understand it. This is often followed by a new message in return, and so the communication process continues.

Although this procedure is always the same, it can take many different forms depending on the type of communication. For example, in non-verbal communication (as opposed to written and spoken communication, which are both verbal), the code used could be gestures, body language, eye contact and facial expressions, such as a smile.

Communication is extremely important in the business world. It is likely that in this context both informal and formal styles will be used. If we take the example of meetings, we might say that they are often conducted in quite a relaxed way, with participants using first names and informal language. However, as soon as the meeting is official, careful records, called minutes, will be kept, following a predetermined format which is standard across many business situations. Layout is one aspect of a formal style. Content will also be dictated to some extent by the level of formality. Annual business reports, for example, must include certain types of information to be legal, such as financial information. Language is another aspect which needs to be taken into account. Formal, written communication needs to be clear and to the point, without spelling or grammar mistakes, and in a formal register (e.g. *Dear ...,* instead of *Hi*). Not following these important rules would have a negative effect in any business context.

Part 3: Exam practice

Questions 1–9

Complete summaries A and B with words from the corresponding passages below. Use NO MORE THAN ONE WORD for each answer.

> **Summary A**
> There should be a small number of (1) _____ at meetings and there needs to be a (2) _____ for any meeting, which will include a clear agenda. During the meeting there needs to be good (3) _____ management and clarity about what the meeting should hopefully (4) _____ . At the end, there should be a summary and agreement about (5) _____ actions.

Passage A

Managers need a range of communication skills to carry out their jobs effectively. They need to be able to articulate their ideas and vision and to convey enthusiasm. Good managers may, at times, need to be able to argue points cogently and to persuade people of their point of view. However, good managers appreciate that communication is a two-way process, and that listening is an important element of communication. Listening to the views of others can help to test ideas as well as to develop new products and methods of production.

The most common forum in which managers are required to communicate are meetings. It is important for managers to draw up a plan for meetings, whether with a single person or with a group. Managers should not invite too many participants to keep numbers to a minimum. They should have a clear agenda for discussion and should exercise tight time controls to prevent meetings dragging on. Managers should enter each meeting with a clear idea of what they want it to achieve. At the end of a meeting, it is good practice to summarize what has been decided and what future steps will be taken and by whom.

> **Summary B**
> Working with other people is not always easy, but it is (6) _____ for the role of managers that they have interpersonal skills that are (7) _____ . Their (8) _____ may need encouragement and help with (9) _____ and solving problems between colleagues.

Passage B

Communication skills should not be taken for granted. Many managers require training in written and oral communication skills and many businesses would benefit from employing managers who speak at least one other language.

Interpersonal skills are also necessary if a manager is to work successfully with other people. If managers lack interpersonal skills, then they are likely to be of limited effectiveness in their role. Managers with effective interpersonal skills can motivate others and can co-ordinate the work of their employees. To do this, managers may need to coach and encourage employees as well as solving disputes and, perhaps more importantly, preventing conflict.

Questions 10–13

Using NO MORE THAN THREE WORDS for each, answer the following questions about passage C.

Exam tip
Training yourself to work against the clock will help you with your timing during the exam.

10 What is the reason that over 10 per cent of international business deals in the UK are not completed?
11 What is a requirement for managers to do their work well?
12 When reading a report, what should managers be able to identify?

Passage C

One criticism of UK managers is that relatively few speak a second language fluently. This can cause obvious problems for businesses that trade in a global market. Research suggests that UK companies lose around 13 per cent of the international deals they try to complete due to 'communication problems'. Managers also need writing skills if they are to carry out their jobs effectively. The ability to quickly summarize key points in the form of a report for others in the business is of real value. So is the skill of reading a report written by someone else and being able to draw out the important elements.

As well as their own staff, managers have to work with other people too. They interact with customers, more senior managers, suppliers, trade union officials, government officials and the local community. Managers need to be comfortable in the company of diverse groups, and they need to able to communicate formally when required and to engage in informal small talk.

Progress Check: Completing notes and summaries

How many boxes can you tick? You should work towards being able to tick them all.

Did you …
remember to use your skim-reading and/or scanning skills to avoid having to read the whole passage? ☐
notice the word limit and stick to it? ☐
try to predict the type of word you were looking for? ☐

Review 2

1 **Answer the following questions about the previous units in NO MORE THAN FIVE WORDS. This will help you practise keeping to word limits.**

   1 What was your favourite topic from units 4–6?
   2 What was the best exam tip you read in these units?
   3 What did you learn about nature from unit 5 that you did not already know?
   4 Have your feelings about the IELTS exam changed since starting to practise with this book? How?

2 **Use these words to complete the text.**

   also   for example   and   such as   although   however

(1) _____ the communication process is always the same, it can take many different forms depending on the type of communication. (2) _____ , in non-verbal communication, the code used could be gestures, body language, eye contact (3) _____ facial expressions, (4) _____ a smile.

From the above examples, it will be clear that communication is not just about the transfer of ideas; it is (5) _____ about feelings and emotions.

In a business context, meetings are often conducted in quite a relaxed way, with participants using first names and informal language. (6) _____ , as soon as the meeting is official, minutes will be kept, following a standard format.

3 **Answer the following questions about the text in exercise 2 by choosing a, b, c or d.**

   1 Where do you think the passage first appeared?
      a in the introduction of an academic article
      b in a beginners' textbook for business students
      c in a general interest magazine aimed at young adults
      d on a website from a business corporation

   2 What was probably the main reason why the writer wrote the text?
      a to inform the reader about the topic of communication
      b to inform the reader about the difficulties of relationships in business contexts
      c to persuade the reader of his/her opinion about communication
      d to question generally held beliefs about business communication

> **Exam tip**
> You will understand a text better if you think about why the writer wrote it and who the text was written for.

4 Match the following words to make collocations that were mentioned in units 4–6.

1 product   a placement
2 coastal   b pursuits
3 public   c history
4 advertising   d town
5 natural   e library
6 women   f agency
7 outdoor   g explorers
8 veterinary   h surgeon
9 marine   i animal

5 Can you name the following objects or animals that you might see on a marine walk?

1 _____ 2 _____ 3 _____ 4 _____

6 Change the wrong word in these sentences so that they are correct.

1 Geology is the science related to the study of living things.
2 A chronometer is an instrument that measures air pressure and shows when the weather is changing.
3 A typical television contains a circuit board, an antenna, a liquid crystal display, a keyboard, a microphone, a speaker and a battery.
4 Evelyn Cheesman was an adventurous scientist who went on many holidays to remote locations and published 16 books.
5 Jellyfish have no eyes, ears, heart or head and are mostly made of bone.
6 Good managers appreciate that communication is a one-way process, and that listening is an important element of communication.

7 Business management

Language development | Vocabulary related to: money
Exam skills | Understanding the function of paragraphs
Exam practice | Matching information

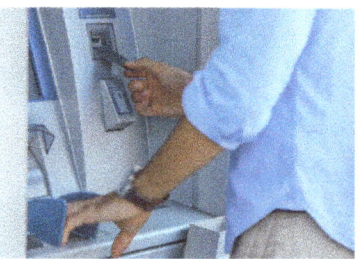

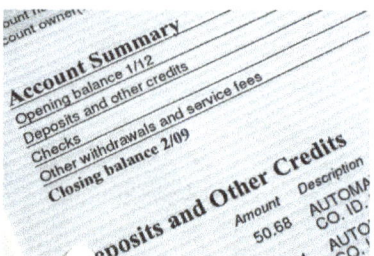

Part 1: Vocabulary

1 Match the words to their definitions.

1	withdrawal	a	money that is immediately available, especially in the form of notes and coins
2	pension	b	an amount of money that you get from your bank
3	bank account	c	a sum of money that you pay to be allowed to do something
4	cash	d	an arrangement with a bank which allows you to keep your money in the bank and to take some out when you need it
5	mortgage	e	a regular sum of money received after retiring (= stopping work completely), given by an employer or by the state
6	bank statement	f	a punishment in which a person is ordered to pay a sum of money because they have done something illegal or broken a rule
7	income	g	the money that a person or organization earns or receives
8	fee	h	a document showing all the money paid into and taken out of a bank account
9	fine	i	a loan of money which you get from a bank in order to buy a house

2a Copy and complete the table on the next page by writing in the words that relate to the categories. Some relate to more than one category.

ATM   withdrawal   cash point   salary   rent   purchase   income
loan   investment   fees   debit card   savings account
fine   mortgage   credit card   owe

Reading for IELTS

Saving money	Borrowing money from the bank	Getting your own money from the bank	Earning money	Paying money

2b Complete these sentences using words from exercise 2a.

1 I have to go to the _____ before we go to the restaurant.
2 If you want to avoid paying a _____, you need to pay your taxes in time.
3 If your children attend private school, you need to pay school _____ .
4 I want to get a new kitchen in the next two years, but I will have to take out a _____ first.
5 When I moved, I took out a _____ over 25 years, but I hope to pay it back early.

> ⚠ **Watch out**
>
> Although *few* and *a few* both mean 'not many', they are used quite differently:
> *few* has a negative meaning. It emphasizes what is missing.
>
> There are **few** copies of this book. = Not many copies exist, so you may not get one.
>
> Note that *few* is normally used in a formal context.
>
> *a few* means, 'a small number'. It emphasizes what is (still) there.
>
> There are **a few** copies of this book. = There aren't many copies but there are some, so you can still have one.

3 Match the sentences 1–2 with their meaning a–b.

1 It should be noted that **there are <u>a few</u> theorists who believe that** this is the right way to do business.

a There are some theorists who believe that.

2 It should be noted that **there are <u>few</u> theorists who believe that** this is the right way to do business.

b It is difficult to find a theorist who believes that.

Part 2: Skills development

ℹ Exam information: Matching information

In the exam, you may be asked to match specific information, for example, a reason, a description or an explanation, to the section of the text where it can be found – A, B, C, etc.

✎ In the paper-based exam, you write the correct letter (A, B, C) next to the number on the answer sheet.

💻 In the online test, the numbered options appear in a table, and you click to highlight the correct column (A, B, C, etc.).

1 Match the underlined parts in the text opposite to the type of specific information. One has already been done for you.

explanation (x3)   reason (x3)   example
comparison   condition

explanation: the companies that are quoted in the leading share price indices

💡 Exam tip

Read the questions first, then skim-read the text to get an idea of its structure, and scan for the specific information. Every paragraph usually has a sentence that summarizes the main idea(s) in the paragraph (the topic sentence). This sentence may help you.

2a What are the following paragraphs about? Choose a, b or c.

1 paragraph A
  a the media
  b large companies
  c smaller businesses

2 paragraph D
  a statistics about India's start-ups
  b the reasons for India's start-up success
  c positive points about India

3 paragraph E
  a the role of policy-makers
  b the importance of business planning
  c tips on improving your business

2b Now decide which sentence in each of the paragraphs A, D and E is the topic sentence.

3 Underline the key words in these questions and then look for the answers in the text.

1 Which paragraph mentions statistics?
2 In paragraph A, which word indicates that the text will not be about large businesses?
3 In paragraph C, who are said to be the people and/or organizations that can make start-ups happen?
4 In paragraph E, which sentences state the benefits of a business plan?

(A) The business sections of the media tend to focus on large, traditional companies. By definition, these are high-profile businesses – the companies that are quoted in the leading share price indices. However, most economists agree that smaller businesses, particularly new and developing small businesses, are central to the long-term success of any economy. They argue that the industries of the future will originate in the small business sector. That is why the SMEs (small and medium-sized enterprises, with less than 250 employees) have been described as 'the engine of economic development'.

(B) Globally, there are about 400 million SMEs, or 90 per cent of all firms, and they provide up to 70 per cent of employment. Although there was a slight drop in the number of SMEs during the COVID-19 pandemic, the numbers have otherwise increased year on year and we now see the best figures ever recorded.

(C) Start-ups are a particular type of small business. The aim of a start-up is typically to bring a new product or service to market, and to grow quickly. The entrepreneurs who start these companies often need funding from investors to start. Governments are also often keen to encourage start-ups, because they can create economic growth, innovation and new jobs. They may do this by giving financial support such as loans or reduced tax.

(D) The United States has the most start-ups, and China and India are also in the top five. India is a particular success story. It currently has over 100,000 start-ups, thanks to its expanding digital economy, young workforce and supportive government schemes. It has a large consumer market, access to global markets and a skilled workforce. Cities such as Bangalore, Delhi and Mumbai are particularly attractive as they have booming technology, finance, media and logistics industries.

Thinking strategically

(E) Policy-makers around the world recognize that it is not sufficient to simply encourage an enterprise culture. If new entrepreneurs are to succeed, if new businesses are to thrive, then it is important that they appreciate the central role of planning. A business plan is the basis of new business development, and it encourages an entrepreneur to think ahead and plan, as far as possible, for the business to be successful. Writing a business plan will not in itself ensure that a business survives. However, it is an invaluable exercise, forcing entrepreneurs to go through planning steps to make sure their business propositions are viable.

share price indices: plural of 'share price index': a system by which (the speed of) changes in the value of share prices is recorded and measured.

Part 3: Exam practice

Questions 1–5

The passage below has eight paragraphs A–H. Which paragraph is about the following information?

1. physical and mental problems that a business owner can face _____
2. leadership and team improvement ideas _____
3. an advantage of not expanding in business _____
4. the reasons why the more basic jobs in a small company should not be not be carried out by employers _____
5. external reasons why companies should try to keep their employees' knowledge and expertise up-to-date _____

Questions 6–8

Complete the summary below with words from paragraphs A and H only. Use NO MORE THAN ONE WORD for each answer.

> Setting up and running a business is not easy. Entrepreneurs need to have a lot of (6) _____, many different skills, and enough (7) _____ to start a company. To make it successful, they need to have a variety of people skills, business management skills, and leadership strategies.
>
> Small business owners also need to know when their successful business has achieved all it can in the format it is in. It can be hard to (8) _____ that developing into a bigger business requires giving over control to others.

Setting up in business

(A) It takes a considerable commitment to set up and run a small business. Owners must be able to do all the tasks necessary to run the business or have sufficient funds to buy in appropriate external help, and even then they must be able to check the quality of the service they are receiving.

(B) Anyone planning to start a business must be realistic about what can be achieved, and in what time frame. Entrepreneurs often work extremely long hours, not just during 'trading' hours, but also after hours doing all the associated paperwork. If entrepreneurs overwork, they will find it difficult to make good decisions and will lack the energy to analyse and evaluate marketing and finance data. If an entrepreneur becomes overtired and overanxious, they can undermine their businesses by giving the impression that things are bad and the business is just about to close down.

(C) Owners need to consider four key issues: training, leadership and team development, delegation and management systems.

(D) Investment in training is necessary to ensure that staff have the skills to do their jobs efficiently and they can meet the requirements of current legislation such as health and safety. Staff may also need training to develop skills to meet internationally recognized quality standards for products and service delivery. Research shows that small and medium-sized firms often find it very difficult to organize effective training.

(E) Ideally, workplace teams should be happy, creative working groups of individuals who support each other, work to each other's strengths and work towards the business's goals. This might require the owners to undertake self-assessment and target-setting reviews to ensure that the business is staying focused on its objectives. Team development can be fostered by organizing events such as team lunches and days out walking together.

(F) Owners should delegate and employ appropriate people to do the tasks that they cannot do or do not have time to do. By freeing themselves from some of the easier day-to-day tasks of the business, owners can spend their time monitoring the overall business and thinking about where the business should be going. Certainly if the owners are passionate about the business, they need time to step back and focus on the long-term goals and vision of the organization. They also need time to network, to build up sales leads and to explore further investment opportunities for the business.

(G) In time, owners need to be able to let go of control of some aspects of the business and to develop more formal management systems. This is probably the most difficult task for any entrepreneur. Many entrepreneurs find it very difficult to trust paid employees to run their businesses.

(H) At this stage in their development, without outside help and guidance, many businesses simply reach their 'natural' capacity and they do not develop or grow any further. Entrepreneurs need to decide whether they want to keep their business small – so that they retain control of all decisions – or whether they want to go on growing their business and therefore accept that this will necessarily change their role in the business.

Progress Check: Matching information

How many boxes can you tick? You should work towards being able to tick them all.

Did you …
remember to identify the key words in the questions? ☐
look for synonyms of the key words? ☐
look for topic sentences in the paragraphs? ☐

8 Arts and literature

Language development | Vocabulary related to: the arts
Exam skills | Understanding sentence structure
Exam practice | Matching sentence endings

Part 1: Vocabulary

1a The following words are related to art as an academic subject: imaginative, creative and non-scientific knowledge that can be studied. Write the words in the correct categories. Use a bilingual dictionary to help you.

| sculpture | poetry | photography | painting | non-fiction | music | jewellery |
| fiction | interior design | directing | dance | architecture | acting |

visual arts	literary arts	performing arts

1b Complete the text with the categories or the words from exercise 1a.

1. Printmaking, drawing, photography and filmmaking are all _____ .
2. I like reading all forms of _____ , e.g. biographies and essays.
3. While many children start with ballet as their first form of _____ , some of them later choose other styles such as modern or ballroom.
4. You can specialise in different aspects of theatre studies in our department, for example acting, playwriting, stage design or _____ .

5 _____ is both an art and a science: it is creative but practicality is also very important. It considers elements such as space, form, light and colour so that people can enjoy the rooms they are in.

6 _____ design is one of the oldest arts, as people have always looked for ways to decorate their bodies. Objects were also made to show wealth, power and belonging.

1c Which categories or words from exercise 1a are being defined?

1 _____: the art of planning, designing and constructing buildings

2 _____: being responsible for the way in which a film, play or television programme is performed, and for telling the actors and assistants what to do

3 _____: books and stories about imaginary people and events, rather than books about real people or events

4 _____: dance, drama, music and other forms of entertainment that are usually performed live in front of an audience

❗ Watch out

In English, sentences usually have a *subject* (often a noun) + a verb:

Architecture   **is**   the art of planning, designing and constructing buildings.
[*noun subject*]   +   [*verb*]

Sometimes, however, there is a longer *noun phrase* before the verb. When you are reading, be careful to look at the whole noun phrase and decide which noun is the main subject.

The staff members who need to speak to the students **are** not here today.
— It is the staff members who are not here, NOT the students (we do not know where they are).

The decision made by the School of Architecture **is** not popular.
— It is the decision that is not popular, NOT the School of Architecture.

2 Read the sentences and answer the questions with the full subject. Then answer the question by underlining the most important noun in the subject.

1 *The photographs of the people partying on the beach with my sisters are really artful.*
Who or what are artful?

2 *The importance of the education I received in the UK should not be forgotten.*
What should not be forgotten?

3 *The details of the art theft that included the royal items of jewellery are not known yet.*
What is not known?

4 *The secret of a successful career, according to my mother, is to study subjects that you care about.*
What is this sentence mainly about: the secret, a career or a mother?

Part 2: Skills development

 Exam information: Matching sentence endings

In the exam, you may be given a number of incomplete sentences and you will need to complete them by choosing from a list of options. There will be more options than you need.

The sentences will be in the same order as the information in the text.

1a Try to predict what type of word will come next in the following sentences. Choose from verb, noun, adjective or preposition. There may be more than one possibility.

1 The Grand Egyptian Museum (GEM) is a national museum located …
2 It is dedicated to Ancient Egypt and its …
3 It invites visitors …
4 Please note that the website visit-gem.com …
5 No outside food or …

 Exam tip

Try to predict how each sentence will end before looking at the list of endings.

1b Now use your predictions to match the sentence beginnings 1–5 above with the correct endings a–e.

1 The Grand Egyptian Museum (GEM) is a national museum located …
2 It is dedicated to Ancient Egypt and its …
3 It invites visitors …
4 Please note that the website visit-gem.com …
5 No outside food or …

a is the only official place to buy online tickets.
b beverages are allowed on the premises
c about 2 kilometres from the Giza Pyramids in Egypt.
d to explore its galleries, shops and exterior gardens.
e culture and society.

Exam tip

Try to predict how each sentence will end before looking at the list of endings. The complete sentences need to accurately reflect the information in the text and be grammatically correct. Focus on the key words in the sentence beginnings and look for synonyms and paraphrases in the text.

2 The text below about sustainable museums has been divided into three parts. There are one or two questions about each part. Choose the best sentence ending from the options.

1 *Museums …*
   a have existed throughout history.
   b help us interpret our surroundings.
   c hold artistic and scientific parties.

2 *The increase in tourism …*
   a will keep increasing in the next decades.
   b has seen museum visitor numbers rise to 100,000.
   c makes us consider its ecological impact.

> Museums play a vital part in the protection and preservation of historical artefacts. By displaying the past, they give generations of visitors the opportunity to make sense of the world around them. However, they represent much more than that. Museums research and celebrate the arts and sciences, educate the public and promote social participation, and thus serve the advancement of society.
>
> With cultural tourism on the rise, the number of museums worldwide is also on the increase and said to be over 100,000. The museum tourism market is worth well over 30 billion US dollars already, and this is predicted to triple in the next ten years.
>
> As with all travel, this raises questions about sustainability: can the needs of tourists be balanced with environmental concerns? According to the World Tourism Organization, tourism is sustainable when it is meaningful to the traveller, economically viable and does not destroy the natural environment or local social structures on which its future depends.

3 *The GEM …*
   a exemplifies sustainable tourism.
   b uses over 60 million litres of river water each year.
   c makes its customers become environmentally friendly travellers.

> In fact, museums can be seen as world leaders in sustainable tourism. The second-largest museum in the world, the Grand Egyptian Museum (GEM), is a good case in point. The museum was the first in Africa and the Middle East with an EDGE Advanced Green Building Certificate. This has been awarded by the IFC, a global development institution. The IFC has praised the museum for its 'energy savings equivalent to removing 400 gasoline-powered vehicles from the streets of Cairo for one year, and water savings equivalent to 63.4 million litres of Nile River water annually'. The museum also promotes eco-tourism to its visitors, hosts environmental programmes and monitors its indoor air quality and noise levels.

4 *The GEM …*
   a organizes talks in schools.
   b protects an international cultural heritage.
   c has a positive influence on nearby businesses.

5 *The GEM …*
   a spends money on hotels and travel.
   b shows artefacts about the environment, culture and finance.
   c cares about both the future and the past.

> The GEM serves as a global model for cultural sustainability too. It collaborates with educational institutions, hosts programmes and workshops, and facilitates discussion about heritage protection. It also produces inclusive educational resources, available to all.
>
> The museum enhances financial sustainability by directly and indirectly providing employment, and in the way it attracts international visitors who contribute to the local economy by spending on retail, food and drink, accommodation and transport.
>
> By combining environmental, socio-cultural and financial sustainability, the museum aims 'to preserve Egypt's unique cultural heritage while contributing to a more sustainable future for generations to come'. This is yet another way in which a museum can contribute to societal progress.

Part 3: Exam practice

Questions 1–5

Based on the information in the text below, complete each sentence with the correct ending A–I.

1 Reading is important to people because ___
2 Reading always involves the readers in an active process because ___
3 Reading can be said to be similar to writing as ___
4 Literature is valued in many cultures because ___
5 Reading is not just a private activity. We know this because ___

A there are a lot of new facts to be found in books.
B it needs technical expertise.
C the UK Department of Education has reported this.
D it documents older views and customs.
E they have to interact both with the content and with the pleasure and other emotions this brings.
F it influences how they feel and learn.
G there are old English, Indian and Japanese stories.
H books are talked about in digital and in-person communities.
I readers also add a lot to a story.

The importance of fiction

Reading is something that matters to everyone: as the UK Department of Education has recently stated, it has an emotional and educational impact on people individually, as well as on society.

Fictional stories in particular can be said to have a strong impact. They allow people to explore the unknown and to learn something new. Readers are not passive participants in a story; they engage with the information in books and with the entertainment they bring. Readers first need to have the technical skills to read and will then use their skills to understand the characters in the story and what motivates them, as well as the way the story develops. For this they need to use their memory and analytical skills. By reading about the characters' experiences they will also share their emotions, such as joy, excitement and sadness.

Readers also need to use their knowledge of the world in order to understand a text and to predict what will come next. In other words, they do not just deconstruct a text but they bring their knowledge and experience to it and help reconstruct its meaning and add their own. Every reader will find something different in the same text and will respond differently to it at different stages in their lives. It could even be argued that a reader's contribution to a story is equal to what the author of the text has put into it.

However, literature is not just important on a personal level: it also has cultural and social importance. Evidence of this can be found in the existence of oral traditions as well as written documents going back centuries. Examples are the classic story of Beowulf, foundational to English literature; the Mahabharata, part of Indian culture and fundamental to Hindu storytelling; and the Japanese Tale of Genji from the 11th century, often called the world's first novel. Stories like these are part of many more traditions around the world, and they form a record and reminder of the values, traditions and languages of their cultures.

More recent evidence of the social importance of stories can be found in book groups, mostly run from people's homes and within their own social circles. Fiction is also discussed all over social media, e.g. in podcasts. All of this shows that stories are (and have always been) meaningful to people: they are shared and discussed and are of personal and cultural significance.

Questions 6–8

Complete the summary below with words from the text. Use NO MORE THAN ONE WORD for each answer.

> Literature has an (6) _____ on all of us who read, and on our communities. One of the ways in which we are affected is emotional, mainly through the way we feel about what happens to the (7) _____ in the stories we read and, arguably, co-create. Culturally and socially, literature is a meaningful part of the human experience, and something that is often (8) _____ online and in person

⇨ Progress Check: Matching sentence endings

How many boxes can you tick? You should work towards being able to tick them all.

Did you …
read the sentence beginnings carefully? ☐
remember to identify the key words in the sentence beginnings? ☐
check carefully if the meaning of the sentence ending you chose corresponded exactly to what was said in the passage? ☐

9 Community matters

Language development | Vocabulary related to: groups
Exam skills | Categorizing
Exam practice | Matching features

Part 1: Vocabulary

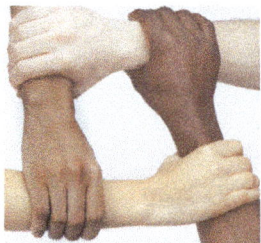   

1   These pictures symbolize different aspects of 'community'. Complete these definitions of two-word phrases where the first word is 'community'. If necessary, choose it from the box below the table.

1 community …	a place that is specially provided for the people, groups and organizations in a particular area, where they can go in order to meet one another and do things
2 community …	a system in which the police work only in one particular area of the community, so that everyone knows them.
3 community …	unpaid work that criminals sometimes do as a punishment instead of being sent to prison
4 community …	help available to people living in their own homes, rather than services provided in residential institutions
5 community …	the feeling of loyalty to a group that is shared by the people who belong to the group

spirit   centre   service   policing   care

2   The word *community* contains information about its meaning and its grammatical category: it is similar to the word *common*, and the -ity ending tells us that the word is a noun.

What do you think the words in the table opposite mean? What are their grammatical categories? If you are not sure, choose from the options in the box below the table.

	grammatical category	meaning
communal		
a commune		
communally		

a together; if things are done or happen in this way, they are shared by everyone in a group

b a group of people who live together and share everything

c belonging or relating to a community as a whole; something that is shared

3 Categorize the following words by ticking the appropriate column(s). There may be more than one correct answer. Then complete the other boxes in the table, where possible.

	adjective	verb	adverb	noun
criminal				
volunteer				
loyalty				
residential				
punish				

4 The words on the right refer to groups of people. Match the words on the left with the words on the right that they best combine with. Use a dictionary if necessary.

1 political
2 online
3 voluntary
4 film
5 rock
6 friendship
7 sports

a party
b cast
c band
d group
e team
f community
g organization

> **⚠ Watch out**
>
> It's important to recognize what pronouns in a text refer to. Be careful with *they*, *their* and *them*: they do not always relate to plural forms. They are often used to talk about individuals instead of using *he*, *she*, *his* or *her*, *him* or *her*.
>
> *A team member must be prepared to put other people's needs before their own.* (This avoids the use of 'his/her own'.)

Part 2: Skills development

ℹ️ Exam information: Matching features

In the exam, you may be asked to match a numbered list of factual statements or opinions to a list of options, which are called 'features' and are identified with letters (A, B, C, etc.). The information in the list of statements will not be in the same order as in the text. You may not need all of the letters or you may be able to use some of them more than once.

1 When matching features, skimming and scanning techniques are useful. Read the text on the next page quickly and then answer the following questions:

1. Which paragraph lists examples of types of volunteering organizations?
2. Which paragraph introduces the roles of volunteering organizations in society?
3. Which paragraph defines what 'third sector' means?
4. Which paragraphs mention theories?
5. Which three theories are mentioned?
6. Which of the three theories is mentioned twice in the text?

💡 Exam tip

In the paper-based exam, it is useful to take notes about where in the passage particular information you are scanning for can be found.

Remember that in the online test, you can insert notes in the text to identify where in the text the information you are looking for can be found. The assessor will not be able to see these.

2 These opinions 1–5 are mentioned in the text. Match them to the correct features A–C. You may use each letter more than once.

1. religious or other values can be a reason for volunteering
2. volunteering improves the well-being of both individuals and society
3. participation in volunteering can lead to more political participation
4. volunteering can encourage togetherness and generosity
5. voluntary organizations are not necessarily good for society

> A the functionalist point of view
> B the conflict theory point of view
> C the symbolic interactionism point of view

64   Reading for IELTS

The Role of Volunteer Organizations

(A) Volunteer organizations play an important role in many communities. In times when many national and local governments are under financial pressure, the need for these organizations to fill the gap is likely to increase. As such they are a key component of civil society.

(B) These organizations, often nonprofit and community-led, range from local food banks and environmental campaigning groups to international humanitarian agencies. Through voluntary participation, they foster social cohesion, encourage civic engagement and contribute to social change.

(C) One of the primary functions of volunteer organizations is providing social services. In many countries, especially where government support may be limited, these organizations offer essential services such as healthcare, education, disaster relief and support for vulnerable populations. Sociologically, this reflects the concept of the 'third sector' – a space distinct from government and private enterprise where citizens participate in collective action for the common good. Volunteer groups often respond more quickly and flexibly to community needs than large institutions, making them crucial in times of crisis.

(D) From a functionalist theory perspective, volunteer organizations contribute to the stability and integration of society. They offer individuals a sense of purpose and identity, help build trust, and reinforce social norms and values through collective action. Volunteering can also serve as a form of informal social control, promoting behaviours that support the well-being of others and discourage isolation and selfishness.

(E) Using the theory of symbolic interactionism, these organizations can be said to have value because of the meanings individuals attach to their volunteer work. Participation in these organizations often reflects deeply held beliefs and values. For example, volunteering at a homeless shelter may not only be an act of service but also an expression of empathy, social responsibility or religious conviction. The micro-level interactions that take place within these groups help form and reinforce group identities and shared understandings.

(F) From a conflict theory perspective, not all volunteer organizations can be seen as promoting social improvements; some may help maintain inequality by doing work that arguably should be the responsibility of the state instead, such as meeting citizens' basic needs.

(G) It has been argued that participation in volunteer organizations is essential for a healthy society: functionalist theory has linked it to larger numbers of people voting in national elections, improved community well-being and stronger social networks.

(H) In short, volunteer organizations are vital to both the everyday functioning and long-term health of society. They offer practical services, create opportunities for civic engagement and shape social identities and norms. While their role is complex and sometimes contested, they remain a cornerstone of collective life.

Part 3: Exam practice

Questions 1–6

Match each item 1–6 with the correct group A–E. You can use a letter for more than one answer.

1. people feel safe here _____
2. people tend to have more money _____
3. it is difficult to say exactly what they are _____
4. they are founded for a specific purpose _____
5. people can do things on a bigger scale _____
6. people are physically close _____

> This is true for:
> A all communities
> B online communities
> C traditional communities
> D meet-up groups
> E none of the mentioned communities

Questions 7–8

Using ONE WORD ONLY for each, answer the following questions.

7. Apart from family, who are also members of close-knit communities? _____
8. How are online communities often unfairly labelled? _____

> **Understanding Community**
>
> The concept of 'community' is complex and can be difficult to define precisely. In general, a community refers to a group of people who share common interests, goals or experiences, which creates a sense of belonging for its members. Communities can take many forms, each offering different benefits.
>
> This chapter explores some types of communities and the common characteristics they share.
>
> **Types of Communities**
>
> One common image of community comes from traditional, rural settings, particularly in developing countries. What sets these traditional communities apart from others, is that their members are not just emotionally close, but also there in person to help each other. Extended families often live together under one roof. Elderly parents may live with their children and grandchildren, which enables the different generations to provide care for each other at the time of need. Neighbours in these communities often play an important role, offering assistance when needed. These tight-knit communities are often viewed as places where, regardless of material wealth, people feel rich in terms of social bonds, as everyone looks out for one another.

At the other end of the spectrum are more modern, sometimes less personal, forms of community, such as online networks. Online communities bring people together from around the world to engage in discussions, share interests and form connections. These communities may not involve face-to-face interactions, and members may never meet in person. Some people view these online relationships as shallow, but digital connections can provide real support and foster strong, meaningful interactions.

In addition to traditional and online communities, there are many other forms of communal involvement. People may join clubs or organizations, participate in political groups or attend local gatherings like coffee mornings or fundraising events. These activities offer a chance to connect with others for both support and collaboration, whether on social, political or personal matters. These meet-up groups are usually set up in response to a need in a particular context.

Common Features of Communities

Despite the diversity in community types, they all share certain characteristics. At their core, communities provide a sense of identity and strength in numbers. Being part of a group helps individuals feel less isolated and more supported. Members of a community know they are part of something larger than themselves and feel connected to people who share similar interests or concerns.

When people come together, they can achieve more than they could on their own. Whether it is gathering information, taking part in team sports or organizing a campaign, collective efforts amplify individual power. In informal communities, such as social or support groups, members also provide emotional backing and a sense of shared experience, which can be invaluable for mental well-being.

The Importance of Community

Communities are vital because they offer members a platform for cooperation, exchange and mutual support. Communities, in all their forms, offer both practical support and a feeling of security. They enable individuals to access resources, gain knowledge and take part in activities that would be difficult to accomplish alone. The sense of belonging that communities provide is crucial for reducing feelings of isolation and enhancing overall happiness.

As social beings, humans have always found ways to organize themselves into groups, whether based on shared geography, interests or experiences. They all fulfil the important function of connecting people, giving them a sense of purpose and collective strength. As society continues to evolve, the importance of community in both physical and virtual spaces will only continue to grow.

Progress Check: Matching features

How many boxes can you tick? You should work towards being able to tick them all.

Did you …
identify the key words in the statements? ☐
look for paraphrases in the text? ☐
scan the text to find the right section? ☐

Review 3

1 Answer the following questions about units 7–9.

1. What was your favourite topic from units 7–9?
2. What was the best exam tip you read in these units?
3. What financial vocabulary can you remember from unit 7?
4. Can you explain the difference between *few* and *a few*?
5. How many nouns can you remember that can go after the word *community*?

2 Find (near) synonyms of the following words in the text below. Try to do this within three minutes. This will help you practise working under timed conditions.

global	importance	develop	supports	help
first	particularly	decline	encourage	vital

The Role of Small and Medium-Sized Enterprises in the Economy

Large multinational corporations such as Starbucks, Apple and Google are often in the news, which can give the impression that they determine the direction of the global economy. Although these companies do contribute significantly to the economy, we should not underestimate the long-term value of small and medium-sized enterprises (SMEs). These businesses not only support the economy in the present but may also evolve into the international brands of the future.

It is this argument which underpins the numerous government schemes and forms of assistance traditionally offered to start-ups – new businesses operating at the local level. These initiatives include financial incentives, reduced business rents and support in drafting business plans. Additional support may involve access to business consultants who assist with initial market research, competitor analysis and company structuring. It is important for our global economy that such support continues, especially in times when public funding is limited.

Entrepreneurs and their start-ups play a vital role during an economic downturn. They are people who provide employment to members of their local communities by identifying market gaps or responding to emerging consumer needs. They promote economic growth by investing not only in their own ventures but also in the people around them.

When local and national governments choose to support new businesses, they are also investing in the broader economic development of the country. The better the support, the greater the likelihood that a business will become one of the 40 per cent that survive their first five years. This kind of investment is particularly crucial during periods of economic uncertainty.

3 Match the beginning and ending of the following sentences. If there is more than one grammatical possibility, think about the meaning.

1 Starbucks and Google are …
2 We need …
3 Entrepreneurs are vital …
4 Support is always important …
5 Every business wants …

a to the economy.
b for employers.
c investment in local businesses.
d to survive their first year in business.
e global brands.

4 Finish the following sentences. You can use your own ideas, as long as the sentence is grammatical. Compare your answers to the complete sentences, which can be found in the text on the opposite page.

1 We should not underestimate …
2 It is this argument which …
3 It is important for …
4 They are people who provide employment to …
5 They promote economic growth by …
6 They are also investing …
7 The better the support, the …

5 Correct the mistakes, if any, in the following sentences.

1 In my community, there are few problems with graffiti, but not very many.
2 If one of my students has disorganized notes, I know they will have problems revising.
3 I dislike it when I have to use a communal bathroom.
4 The person who is standing next to my sister is taller than her, but only because they are wearing a hat.

6 Label the following pictures. They are all two-word phrases from unit 9. The first two refer to groups, the third to an activity.

1 _____ 2 _____ 3 _____

Review 3

10 Back in time

Language development | Vocabulary related to: history
Exam skills | Understanding text organization; Understanding the topic of paragraphs
Exam practice | Matching headings

Part 1: Vocabulary

1   The following phrases relate to the topic of history. Fill in the missing vowels.

visit a m__s__ __m   a national tr__d__t__ __n
in r__c__nt years   A historical d__c__m__nt

2a Are the words in the box nouns or adjectives? Copy the table and write the words **in bold** in the right categories.

long **period**	**historical** event	new **era**	**former** president	**modern** life
ancient city		20th **century**	famous **historian**	

nouns	adjectives

Glossary
era: You can refer to a period of history or a long period of time as an era when you want to draw attention to a particular feature or quality that it has, e.g. *the digital era*. The word *period* is a more general.

Unit 10

2b Fill in the gaps in the text with the words that are in bold in the box

The Aztec Empire

The Aztecs were a powerful people who lived in (1) _____ Mexico. Their empire grew strong during the (2) _____ from the 14th to the 16th (3) _____ They built their capital, Tenochtitlán, on a lake and created a large empire through war and alliances.

This (4) _____ of Aztec rule ended in 1521 when Spanish soldiers took over the land. The (5) _____ capital city was destroyed, but many parts of Aztec culture still live on in (6) _____ Mexico.

The Aztecs are remembered today for their buildings, religion and influence on Mexican food, language and festivals.

Glossary
alliance: a formal agreement between two or more countries or political parties to work together

3 Match the words to their definitions

1. an archive
2. an artefact
3. a monument
4. a ruin

a. something that was built to remember an event or person
b. a collection of documents or other evidence
c. a part of a building that remains after the rest has fallen down
d. something made by human beings, such as a tool or a work of art

⚠ Watch out

The way time periods are described can be a little confusing:
- Centuries describe the previous time period. For example, the 18th century started in **17**01 and ended in 1800; the **21**st century started in **20**01 and will end in 2100.
- BC (Before Christ) and BCE (Before Common Era) refer to the same period, the years up to year 1
- AD (Anno Domino) and CE (Common Era) refer to the same period, starting at year 1
- Many historians now use BCE and CE
- 10BCE is earlier than 5BCE, but 5CE is earlier than 10CE!

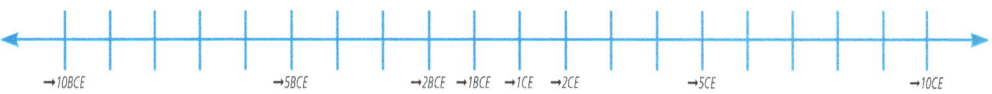

→10BCE   →5BCE   →2BCE →1BCE →1CE →2CE   →5CE   →10CE

Back in time 71

Part 2: Skills development

> **ⓘ Exam information: Matching headings**
>
> In the exam, you may be given a list of headings, and a text divided into sections. The headings will be in the form of short statements which summarize the information in a section. You will need to read the text sections and decide which of the headings best fits that section. This type of task tests whether you understand the organization of texts and can identify the main idea or topic in a paragraph.

1a To focus on this type of task, underline the main point in box A (the introduction). Then check your answer in the key before continuing.

1b Read all the paragraphs that follow and underline any evidence that links to this main point. Notice how one main theme is developed throughout the text.

1c Explain how the meaning of each of the following phrases is related to the overall theme of the text. The first one is done for you.

> *moreover (in A): introduces another reason why it is difficult to compare styles/periods*
>
> first of all (in B)   secondly (in B)   last but not least (in B)
> despite (in C)   then again (in C)   moreover (in C)
> unsurprisingly (in D)

1d We can say that each of the paragraphs B–D exemplifies the general theme with an example of a particular period. What is the example in each of these paragraphs?

1e The text has no conclusion. Look at the following suggestions for the conclusion of this text and cross out any that are not suitable.

The conclusion could:

   a pick up the point about how easy it is to be confused (i.e. the fact that different words refer to the same period and that the same words can refer to different periods)

   b refer back to the three main examples in paragraphs B–D

   c mention that non-British people may find it harder to understand the vocabulary relating to artistic styles

   d give information about another period (e.g. introduce the Elizabethan period)

   e include a personal opinion or comment relating to the main idea, or its consequences (e.g. visitors to the UK may need more information about tourist attractions than we might think)

> **A**
> It is not easy to compare the artistic styles and periods of different countries, especially as they may use different words to refer to the same features, and perhaps occasionally also use the same words with a slightly different meaning. Moreover, particular styles and periods overlap.

B

An example of this is the 'Victorian' period in Britain, which has a style that is often described as romantic. First of all, the name of this period links it immediately with British royal history, which potentially creates confusion to non-British people who may not be aware that the reign of Queen Victoria relates to approximately the second half of the 19th century. Secondly, despite the fact that Queen Victoria died in 1901 the style itself continued into the 20th century. And last but not least, it can be argued that there are distinctly different styles which can all be referred to as Victorian, e.g. the use of flower motifs and pastel colours.

C

Despite Victorian times being characterized by romanticism, the famous British romantic poets belong to the period before Queen Victoria. These are poets such as Robert Burns, William Wordsworth, Samuel Taylor Coleridge and John Keats. From the same era date famous writers such as Jane Austen and Mary Shelley (who wrote Frankenstein), and great architects such as James Wyatt and John Nash. The great painters Gainsborough, Reynolds, Turner and Constable can also be categorized in this period. But who outside of Britain could label this era? And, even if we know they can all be described as Georgian artists, which King George does this refer to? Actually, it refers to four of them (George I, George II, George III and George IV), and thus spans a long period incorporating most of the 18th century and some of the 19th. But then again, there was a Georgian revival in the 20th century, which means the label can also relate to that. Moreover, the style itself incorporates previous styles, including gothic, and has its own subdivision, Regency style, which describes the period of George IV.

D

The period after the Victorian era is referred to as Edwardian, after Edward VII who reigned from 1901 to 1910, when he died. Nobody is sure whether 1910 is the correct end point for the period, with some people suggesting it should be 1912, when the Titanic sank, the start of World War I (1914), its end (1918), or the signing of the post-war peace treaty of Versailles (1919). Elsewhere in Europe, the Art Nouveau era ended around the same time, and unsurprisingly, Art Nouveau is also used to describe the style which was common in Britain at that time. Floral motifs were very common … now where have I heard about that before?

2 Read the following paragraphs about British castles. Choose the best heading from the options.

Beaumaris Castle is an impressive castle, built by King Edward I. It is considered one of the most beautiful medieval castles in Wales, probably because of its symmetrical shapes, but its purpose was military, the pretty geometrical shapes being rings of defence. Work started as early as 1295, but although it was done at a fast speed, it was never completed because of lack of money.

Scotland is right to be proud of Edinburgh Castle. It dominates the city of Edinburgh from high up on its rock. The history of Castle Rock goes back all the way to the late Bronze Age (900 BC), when there were already people living there. In the Middle Ages it became a royal castle, and this lasted until the 17th century. In the 18th century it became an army base, but it is now mainly known as a visitor attraction.

a Beaumaris: a castle of contrasts
b Beaumaris: a typical medieval castle
c Beaumaris: the oldest Welsh castle

a Is Edinburgh the oldest castle in Britain?
b Edinburgh Castle: 1,000 years of history
c Edinburgh Castle and its many roles

Part 3: Exam practice

Questions 1–5

The reading passage has five sections A–E. Choose the correct heading for sections A–E from the list of numbered headings below. Write the correct number 1–8 next to sections A–E.

List of headings	Sections
1 Medicine and Education	Section A: _____
2 Law	Section B: _____
3 Technology	Section C: _____
4 Religion and Culture	Section D: _____
5 Language	Section E: _____
6 Urban Planning	
7 Politics	
8 Architecture and Engineering	

Questions 6–7

Multiple choice: choose the appropriate letter a, b, or c.

6 Where is the Latin language still used today?

  a in academic and religious writing
  b in Europe, the Americas and parts of Africa
  c in Western educations systems

7 Which of these is a Roman symbol?

  a Christianity
  b national emblem
  c eagle

The Roman Empire and its continuing impact

The Roman Empire, which lasted from 27 BCE to 476 CE in the West and until 1453 CE in the East (the Byzantine Empire), was one of the most influential civilizations in world history. Although it had its centre in Europe, its influence has extended far beyond its original borders, and art, culture and systems across continents. The Roman Empire's influence continues to resonate globally.

Section A
Roman legal traditions laid the groundwork for many modern systems. The civil model, derived from Roman principles, is used today in much of Europe, Latin America and parts of Africa. Countries like Japan and South Korea adopted similar legal systems during modernization. Even the US Constitution reflects Roman ideas of republicanism and civic duty. These principles have helped shape governance structures across the globe.

Section B
Latin, the language of the Romans, evolved into the Romance languages – Spanish, Portuguese, French, Italian and Romanian – which are spoken across Europe, the Americas and parts of Africa. Latin also left a deep imprint on English vocabulary, especially in law, science and medicine. In Asia, Latin terminology is used in academic and medical contexts, particularly in India and the Philippines, where Western education systems were introduced during colonial periods. The global use of Latin in religious and scholarly contexts continues to this day.

Section C
Structures around the globe have been inspired by Roman innovation. In North America, buildings like the US Capitol and Supreme Court reflect Roman neoclassical design. In South America, colonial cities such as Lima and Buenos Aires feature Roman-inspired arches and columns. Roman aqueducts influenced Spanish infrastructure, which was later replicated in Mexico and Peru. Even in Australia, public buildings in Canberra show neoclassical elements rooted in Roman design.

Section D
Roman cities were known for their organized layouts, public forums and advanced sanitation systems. London, originally the Roman city of Londinium, still retains elements of its Roman layout. In North Africa, Roman ruins in cities like Tunis and Tripoli are integrated into modern urban life. Roman road-building techniques influenced colonial infrastructure in India and South Africa, where straight, durable roads facilitated administration and trade. The Roman model of city planning continues to be used worldwide.

Section E
The Roman Empire played a central role in the spread of Christianity, which became the empire's official religion in the 4th century. From Europe, Christianity spread to the Americas, Africa, Asia and Oceania through colonization and missionary work. Ethiopia adopted Christianity early and remains predominantly Christian. In the Philippines, Spanish colonization introduced Catholicism, making it the largest Christian nation in Asia. Roman religious traditions and festivals continue to shape cultural calendars across continents. Roman symbols – eagles, laurel wreaths and togas – appear in national emblems from Mexico to Indonesia, reflecting Rome's enduring cultural prestige.

Progress Check: Matching headings

How many boxes can you tick? You should work towards being able to tick them all.

Did you …
- skim-read the sections first, one by one? ☐
- identify key words? ☐
- consider the main point of each paragraph? ☐
- consider the overall text organization? ☐

11 Crime detection

Language development | Vocabulary related to: crime
Exam skills | Identifying information; Adjusting reading speed
Exam practice | True/False/Not Given questions

Part 1: Vocabulary

1 The pictures relate to the process of solving crimes. Match the words and phrases from the box to the pictures.

fingerprint   DNA evidence   suspect   surveillance

1 _____ 2 _____ 3 _____ 4 _____

2a Match these verbs with their meanings.

1	witness	a	to use science to examine something
2	suspect	b	to take someone away because they are believed to have done something illegal
3	arrest	c	to state in court what someone's punishment will be
4	analyse	d	to believe that something unpleasant or wrong has been done
5	report	e	to punish someone by making them pay money because they have done something illegal or broken a rule
6	search	f	to look for something
7	charge	g	to see something happen
8	sentence	h	to formally state that someone has done something illegal
9	fine	i	to tell people about something

2b Most of the verbs from exercise 2a have the same form as a noun, e.g. *suspect*: the police may have a *suspect* (noun), or they might *suspect* (verb) someone of committing a crime.

For one of these words 1–9, the noun has a different form from the verb. Which one?

> **Exam tip**
>
> Notice the part of speech of a word when reading; ask yourself whether the word is a noun, verb, adjective, etc. For certain exam type questions (e.g. text, note or diagram completion) you will need to be able to identify what the part of speech of a word is in its context.

Unit 11

2c Use words 1–9 from exercise 2a to fill in the correct nouns in the text.

Last night, a (1) _____ came forward with important information about a robbery. She had seen the (2) _____ near the scene just minutes before the crime. The police quickly began a (3) _____ of the area and found several clues. Later, they made an (4) _____, and questioned the suspect for many hours. A full (5) _____ was written, and the case will likely go to court soon.

2d Fill in the correct preposition. Choose from: *with, to, for, on*.

1 The woman was arrested _____ suspicion of theft.
2 He was charged _____ robbery after the investigation
3 The police searched _____ the stolen items in the suspect's house.
4 She was fined _____ parking illegally in a no-parking zone.
5 The man was sentenced _____ five years in prison.
6 A witness came forward and reported the crime _____ the police.

3 In this text about the criminal justice system, underline the words which are related to crime, e.g. the work done by the police and the courts. Use a dictionary to help you.

When a crime has been committed, police go to the crime scene to look for clues. They collect evidence like fingerprints, blood or objects left behind. This is part of forensics, which helps solve the case.

If the evidence shows someone did the crime, the police can prosecute them in court. A lawyer will try to prove the person is guilty. If the court decides the person is guilty, they are convicted and may go to prison. But if there isn't enough proof, the person will be found innocent.

Part 2: Skills development

ℹ Exam information: True/False/Not Given

In the exam, you may be asked whether information is correct or not. You will be given a list of statements. If the text confirms the statement, your answer should be 'TRUE'. If the text contradicts the statement your answer should be 'FALSE'. If it is impossible to know from the text if the statement is true or not, your answer should be 'NOT GIVEN'.

Do not use your own opinion to answer but check in the text.

1 Do the sentences on the left provide answers to the questions on the right? Put a tick when they do, or write NOT GIVEN if they don't. Use only the information in the statements.

Sentences	Questions	✓ or NOT GIVEN
Fingerprints have been found that date back thousands of years to the time of the ancient Egyptians.	1 Do we have computers that help us determine how old fingerprints are?	
	2 Did the ancient Egyptians live thousands of years ago?	
In 1910, Edmond Locard set up what is thought to be the first police crime laboratory in Lyons in France.	3 Is Edmond Locard French?	
	4 Is Lyons in France?	
DNA fingerprinting was first used in the 1980s when it was used as evidence to convict murderer Colin Pitchfork.	5 Was DNA fingerprinting technically possible in 1990?	
	6 Did Colin Pitchfork commit murder?	

2 Read the statements below and write TRUE if the text next to it confirms the information, FALSE if it contradicts the information, or NOT GIVEN if there is not enough information.

Text	Statements	TRUE/FALSE/ NOT GIVEN
The paralegals (PLs) who assist in preparing legal documents and researching and organizing case materials are employed by law firms but are not lawyers.	1 PL means paralegal.	
	2 Researching case materials is crucial work.	
	3 Paralegals assist lawyers in court.	
The PL work involves tight deadlines and the need for precision, since even minor errors can have serious legal consequences.	4 Paralegal work is difficult to do.	
	5 The PL job requires attention to detail.	
	6 PLs work late to meet deadlines.	

3 Make a note of your starting time. Read Part 1 as fast as you can, but make sure you understand what you read. Do not stop for unknown vocabulary. Then check your understanding by answering the questions. Make a note of the time when you finish.

Then do the same for Part 2. Check if you managed to complete Part 2 faster than Part 1.

Surveillance and society: the use of CCTV (Part 1)

Closed-circuit television (CCTV) systems have become a defining feature of modern urban life across the globe. From the busy streets of Tokyo to the public squares of São Paulo, surveillance cameras are now widely used to monitor public spaces, deter crime and support law enforcement.

CCTV has been credited with reducing certain types of crime, particularly in high-traffic areas like transportation hubs, shopping centres and nightlife districts. There is evidence that it is helpful in reducing shoplifting and car crime. It has also helped identify terrorists and murderers.

However, many claim that effective lighting is just as effective to prevent crime, and that cameras could simply displace crime. Most schemes that simply record city centres continually – often not being watched – do not produce results. CCTV can also have the opposite effect of that intended, by giving citizens a false sense of security and encouraging them to be careless with property and personal safety.

True, False, or Not Given?

1 Tokyo uses surveillance technology in its law enforcement efforts.
2 CCTV has helped solve crimes on public transport.
3 CCTV can make people feel safe, which puts them in more danger.

Surveillance and society: the use of CCTV (Part 2)

In response, cities such as Singapore, Seoul and Toronto have integrated CCTV into broader public safety strategies, combining it with real-time monitoring and emergency response systems.

The global spread of CCTV has also raised important ethical and legal questions. In democratic societies, concerns about privacy, data protection and government power are central to the debate. Citizens and advocacy groups often question how footage is stored, who has access to it and whether surveillance is being used proportionately.

Despite these challenges, the use of CCTV continues to grow, driven by advances in artificial intelligence, cloud storage and smart city infrastructure. This global growth is also supported by public demand for safer streets, faster emergency response and more efficient policing. Finding the right balance between public safety and individual rights remains an important challenge for governments, technology experts and communities around the world.

True, False, or Not Given?

1 In Seoul, there are people who watch CCTV images while they happen.
2 Citizens and advocacy groups have asked for access to CCTV footage.
3 The public wants better protection, e.g. by the police.

Part 3: Exam practice

> **Exam tip**
> You should adjust your reading speed throughout the exam. When you are looking for detailed information (e.g. the writer's opinion), you will need to slow down to make sure you find the exact answer. When you are asked for more general information (e.g. matching paragraph headings), you may be able to read faster. By practising, you will find the ideal balance between reading slowly enough to understand and fast enough to finish on time.

Questions 1–6

Choose TRUE if the statement agrees with the information given in the text below, choose FALSE if the statement contradicts the information, or choose NOT GIVEN if there is no information on this.

1 The police may ask the people who are at the crime scene to wait together until they can talk to them. _____
2 SOCOs are not normally first at a crime scene. _____
3 Sometimes hair, skin cells, etc. from a SOCO are left at the crime scene, even though they wear protection to try to stop this. _____
4 Every item at a crime scene is photographed five times. _____
5 Fibres are an example of trace evidence. _____
6 If evidence is burnt, it cannot be dealt with. _____

Questions 7–8

Choose the correct heading for sections C and E. Choose from:

Photographing the scene. _____
Hunting for clues. _____
Storing types of evidence. _____
Recording the scene. _____
The SOCO's role. _____

Investigating a crime scene

A

On arrival, the police officer's first job is to carry out an initial assessment of the scene. If they are at first unsure whether or not a crime has taken place, it's best to assume that it has. Valuable time and evidence in the investigation could be lost otherwise. First they must deal with anyone at the scene needing medical help. Any other people present at the scene must be kept apart, as they may be eyewitnesses or suspects. Witnesses at crime scenes are not allowed to talk to each other. A person's perception of what happened can get distorted during conversation.

The police officer then calls for a Scene of Crime Officer (SOCO).

B

When the SOCO arrives at the crime scene, they put on a full protective body suit, gloves, a mask and plastic overshoes. Without this, the SOCO's skin cells, hair, fibres, fingerprints or shoeprints could be added to the crime scene.

C

The SOCO must produce a permanent record of the crime scene, using detailed written notes, sketches, photographs and videos. It is essential that the original position of items at the scene is recorded. Some biological and chemical evidence may quickly deteriorate. Other evidence may be very fragile, and might be destroyed as the SOCO tries to recover it. Other evidence from the scene of crime will be sent to the forensic lab for analysis.

D

When photographing a crime scene, the SOCO follows four rules:

1 Photograph the whole crime scene.
2 Photograph each item at the scene before doing anything to it.
3 Add a scale and photograph the item again.
4 After collecting trace evidence from the item, photograph the same part of the crime scene again.

E

Any evidence at the crime scene may turn out to be important at some stage in the investigation, so it's important that the team's search is thorough and systematic.

- Some of the evidence, such as a cigarette butt, may be immediately obvious to the SOCO.
- Some of the evidence, such as fibres, may be present in very small amounts. This is called trace evidence.
- Other evidence, such as fingerprints, may be invisible to the naked eye, and special techniques are needed to reveal it.
- Some evidence may have been damaged, for example burnt. Special procedures are then needed.

Progress Check: Identifying information

How many boxes can you tick? You should work towards being able to tick them all.

Did you ...
think about your reading speed and adjust it if necessary? ☐
focus on detail? A general topic can be mentioned but the answer can still be *Not Given* if the ☐
exact information is not in the text.

12 Travel

Language development | Vocabulary related to: places and travel
Exam skills | Formal and informal phrases; Working with paraphrases; Distinguishing between fact and opinion; Identifying information
Exam practice | Yes/No/Not Given questions

Part 1: Vocabulary

1 Label the pictures.

pavement   junction   traffic lights   crossing

1 _____ 2 _____ 3 _____ 4 _____

2 Match the British English words with their American English equivalents on the right.

1 pavement/footpath   a intersection
2 junction   b stop lights/traffic signals
3 traffic lights   c sidewalk
4 crossing   d license plate
5 car park   e gas/gasoline
6 petrol   f parking lot
7 motorway   g freeway/interstate
8 lorry   h crosswalk
9 number plate   i truck
10 diversion   j detour

3 Use the information in the text to write your own definitions for the words in bold.

> Before any international trip, it's helpful to prepare an **itinerary** that outlines your travel plans and scheduled activities. Many leisure travellers include at least one **excursion** – a short trip to a nearby location of interest – which can offer unique cultural or historical experiences beyond the main **destination**. For instance, someone visiting Athens might also plan an excursion to Delphi or the islands nearby. Equally important is ensuring that all **travel documentation** is complete and up to date. This includes passports, visas, vaccination records and any required travel insurance or booking confirmations.

Unit 12

4a The table shows words and phrases that give information about what the writer thinks.

Put the headings in the correct columns:
- expressing facts
- expressing probability or certainty
- expressing opinions

presumably probably possibly	supposedly arguably allegedly	undoubtedly evidently actually
it seems unlikely that it is difficult to believe that there is a chance that	from my point of view as far as I am concerned I would say that	in fact it is true that it is a known fact that

4b Which of the words in the first row of the table above do people use when:

1. they think something is likely to be the case but they are not certain (3 possible answers)
2. they talk about something bad which other people say is true, but there is no proof (1 answer)
3. they want to give more authority to their opinion or belief (1 answer)
4. they are certain about something (2 answers)
5. they give a surprising opinion or an opinion that contradicts someone else's (1 answer)

❗ Watch out

Do not confuse the following words:
- ***Probably*** and ***possibly*** do not have the same meaning. If someone is more than 50% sure, they would use *probably*, if they are less than 50% sure, they would use *possibly*.
- ***Apparently*** is used to give information based on what someone else has said; ***obviously*** is based on actual evidence.

Part 2 Skills development

> ### ℹ Exam information: Yes/No/Not Given
>
> In the exam, you may be asked to demonstrate that you understand the points of view expressed in a text. You will be given a list of statements which each represent an opinion. You have to read the text to find out if the writer expresses these opinions or not. If the writer shares the opinion in the statement, your answer will be YES. If the writer contradicts the statement, your answer will be NO. If it is impossible to know from the text what the writer's opinion is about that subject, your answer will be NOT GIVEN.
>
> The information in the text will be in the same order as the list of statements.

1 It is important to understand the difference between facts and opinions. An opinion does not have to be based on fact or knowledge and we cannot prove it right or wrong.

Are the following statements facts or opinions?

1. The distance between Bologna and Florence is about 100 kilometres. _____
2. There are currently two areas with roadworks between Bologna and Florence. _____
3. Florence organizes a yearly carnival and a music festival, both of which attract international audiences. _____
4. Florence is well worth a visit. _____
5. Florence and Bologna are both rich in architecture and art, but Bologna is less touristy. _____
6. You can't get from Bologna to Florence in less than an hour unless you break the speed limit. _____
7. Bologna has better clothes shops than Florence. _____

2a Read the texts and the statements that follow them. Write YES if the opinion is expressed in the text (= the writer agrees) and NO if the writer disagrees.

> Public transport is often praised for being efficient and environmentally friendly. However, it does not always meet the needs of all users. In rural areas, services may be infrequent or unavailable, making private vehicles essential. Even in cities, delays and overcrowding can discourage regular use. While cycling and walking are sustainable alternatives, they are not practical for everyone. A more effective approach would be to improve public transport reliability while supporting flexible options like car-sharing and electric vehicles. Encouraging greener travel should not mean ignoring the diverse needs of commuters.

1. People are generally aware that public transport helps protect the planet. _____
2. Some passengers are not satisfied with the level of service that public transport provides. _____
3. It is possible to rely on public transport only. _____
4. Nothing is more important than achieving eco-friendly transport. _____

> Instead of complaining about roadworks, the cost of petrol, the price of cars, etc. we need to think about other options. And I don't mean car sharing or building more motorways. I say we try to save our environment by campaigning for better bus and train networks and for different types of transport, such as trams.

5 We should complain about car-related problems. _____
6 The environment is not really in danger. _____
7 Public transport needs to be improved. _____

> The world's dependency on fuel is something that should concern us all. Here are just some examples of the consequences when prices rise. Elderly people cannot afford to heat their houses, people lose their jobs because they can no longer afford to commute to work, or because they are made redundant from their jobs in transport-based businesses such as airlines. Self-employed people often rely on their own transport for work, e.g. delivery people, florists and taxi drivers, so they may be forced to close their businesses. The prices of some food and raw materials also increase as a direct result of the cost of oil, e.g. the prices of beef and cotton.
>
> One promising development in response to this is the growing popularity of electric vehicles (EVs) with consumers: they reduce oil dependence, produce fewer emissions and are easy to charge at home. They also provide a quiet and comfortable ride. Although challenges remain – such as limited charging infrastructure and concerns over battery production – investment in EVs could help reduce both economic pressure and environmental harm.

8 We need to worry about our overreliance on fuel. _____
9 There are more problems caused by increasing fuel prices than the ones mentioned in the passage. _____
10 The price of beef is closely related to the price of oil. _____
11 People buy EVs because they offer practical benefits, environmental benefits and a good driving experience. _____

2b Notice how synonyms and paraphrases were often used in the statements. For each statement in exercise 2a, underline the word(s) in the text that helped you.

3 Look back at the third passage in exercise 2a. Are the following ideas in the text (✓) or are they NOT GIVEN?

1 Old people may die because they cannot keep warm. _____
2 There is more unemployment when fuel prices rise. _____
3 People who deliver goods may use their personal vehicles to do this. _____
4 The price of corn and corn-based foods are related to the price of oil. _____
5 EVs are easy to maintain. _____

💡 Exam tip
To help you determine if something is NOT GIVEN, look for synonyms and paraphrases. If none appear, the answer will probably be NOT GIVEN. But even if you do find paraphrases, be careful: it may be that the topic is mentioned but not in relation to the statement.

Part 3: Exam practice

 **Exam tip**

Throughout the exam, you need to make sure you rely on the information in the passages, not on your own ideas. This is especially important with this type of question: never be tempted to reflect your own opinion, always consider only what is in the text.

Questions 1–6

Read the following passage. Do the statements agree with the views of the writer? Write:

YES	if the statement agrees with the views of the writer
NO	if the statement contradicts what the writer thinks
NOT GIVEN	if it is impossible to know what the writer's point of view is

1 Another name for the East–West trading route is 'Silk Road'. _____
2 Zhang Qian is admired by Chinese schoolchildren. _____
3 Zhang Qian was a Chinese adventurer. _____
4 At least one German used the Silk Road in the 19th century. _____
5 Silk was the main material to be traded on this route. _____
6 The Silk Road was used for trade in natural materials, man-made materials and animals. _____

Questions 7–9

Choose three letters from A–I. The list below gives some facts and opinions about the Silk Road. Which THREE of these are expressed by the writer of the text?

A items transported on the route included glassware, gemstones and tea ___
B The Romans are likely to have used the Silk Road ___
C the Stone Tower is located either in the Pamir region, or the Alay Valley ___
D for thousands of years, all the trade was recorded ___
E the route helped spread ideas and technologies ___
F traders traditionally exchanged goods in Kashgar ___
G in order to successfully complete the journey, timing was essential ___
H traders had to travel across the Taklaman desert ___
I The Silk Road is 800 miles long ___

Schoolchildren in China learn that the opening of the East–West trading route popularly known as the Silk Road occurred in 139 BC when Zhang Qian, the Chinese ambassador-adventurer, travelled westward across the Pamirs, a mountain range in Central Asia. He was the first known Chinese person to do so. The term 'Silk Road' was actually first used late in the nineteenth century by a German geographer, Baron Ferdinand von Richthofen (1833–1905). Silk was not the only material that passed along these routes. Other goods are known to have included ceramics, glass, precious gems and livestock.

However, there are reasons to think that these roads were being used centuries, probably even millennia, earlier than Zhang's expedition. In Roman times, Pliny the Elder reported a 'stone tower' which he said existed on the Pamir Plateau where goods had been traditionally exchanged between traders from the East and the West. In the early second century, Maës Titianus, an ancient Roman-Macedonian traveller, actually reported reaching this famous stone tower, but its exact location remains uncertain. According to one theory, it was at Tashkurgan in the Pamirs. (The word 'Tashkurgan' actually means 'stone tower' or 'stone fortress' in the Uyghur language.) Scholars today, however, believe that its location was probably somewhere in the Alay Valley. Whatever the truth about the stone tower may be, it seems likely that some form of trade was taking place in this region millennia before more formal recorded trade took place.

On the other hand, it is difficult to believe that people in those times were able to travel such huge distances. Travelling from West to East, the trader first had to cross the Pamir Plateau, through the 20,000-foot-high mountains. If the weather in the mountains had been kind and the journey undertaken in the right season, the eastward-bound traveller would then finally arrive at Kashgar, a logical place for trade and rest, where they could exchange horses or camels and then start on the return journey back over the mountains before the winter snows started.

It is unlikely that in these earlier times traders or travellers would have continued further eastwards from Kashgar, as they would have had to go round the Taklamakan Desert. Going through it was not an option as its name suggests: it literally means 'Go in and you won't come out'. Beyond this desert, there still would have remained 800 miles of a dangerous journey before they would have found the first true signs of Chinese civilization.

Adapted from *The Moon over Matsushima – Insights into Mugwort and Moxa*, by Merlin Young (Godiva Press).

Progress Check: Identifying writers' view or claims

How many boxes can you tick? You should work towards being able to tick them all.

Did you …
remember that the questions are in the same order as the information in the text? ☐
base your answers on the text, not on your own opinion? ☐
look for synonyms and paraphrases in the text? ☐
focus on detail to make sure that the information in the statement related to exactly what was in the passage? ☐

Review 4

1 Answer or think about the following questions about units 10–12.

1 What was your favourite topic from units 10–12?
2 What was the best exam tip you read in these units?
3 What crime-related vocabulary can you remember from unit 11?
4 Which century were you born in? And your grandparents?
5 Which job would you prefer to do: someone who monitors CCTV, a paralegal or a SOCO? Why?
6 Has there been any change in how confident you feel about the IELTS reading exam?

2 Write the adjectives for each of these words. The adjectives all appeared in units 10–12.

1 history _____
2 law _____
3 globe _____
4 medicine _____
5 religion _____
6 tourism _____
7 electricity _____
8 possibility _____

3 Complete the gaps with the correct form of the word between brackets.

Beaumaris Castle

Beaumaris Castle is an **(1)** (impress) _____ **(2)** (middle ages) _____ castle. It was built by King Edward I and is considered one of the most **(3)** (beauty) _____ castles in Wales, probably because of its **(4)** (symmetry) _____ shapes, but its purpose was military. Work started in 1295, but although it was **(5)** (do) _____ at a fast speed, it was never completed because of lack of money.

Scotland is right to be **(6)** (pride) _____ of Edinburgh Castle. It **(7)** (dominate) _____ the city of Edinburgh from high up on its rock. The history of Castle Rock goes back all the way to the late Bronze Age (900 BC), when there were already people **(8)** (live) _____ there. It is now **(9)** (main) _____ known as a **(10)** (visit) _____ attraction. Although it is more **(11)** (expense) _____ than other tourist attractions, people visit it because it offers **(12)** (excellence) _____ value.

Edinburgh Castle

4 Fill in the missing words in these sentences:

1 The woman was _____ on suspicion of theft.
2 He was _____ with robbery after the investigation.
3 The police _____ for the stolen items in the suspect's house.
4 She was _____ for parking illegally in a no-parking zone.
5 The man was _____ to five years in prison.
6 A witness came forward and _____ the crime to the police.

5 Complete the gap with the most appropriate adverbs. Choose from *supposedly*, *possibly* and *arguably*.

> Japan is a country that offers a unique blend of tradition and modernity. Those planning a trip will definitely want to visit in spring when the cherry blossoms are in full bloom, but there could (1) _____ be local festivals in summer too.
> Tokyo is (2) _____ one of the most exciting cities in the world, known for its cutting-edge technology, traditional arts and world-class cuisine.
> For a more rural feel, many tourists visit Mount Fuji. The small town of Aokigahara, located near Mount Fuji, is (3) _____ haunted, although there are very few reports of visitors seeing ghostly activity.

6 For each of these sentences, write BE if they contain at least one word that is only used in British English, and AE if they contain one only used in American English. Do you know the equivalent word? Some of the words were used in Unit 12, others may be new to you.

1 We have bought a new faucet for the kitchen in a black color. _____
2 When we are away, our neighbor puts the garbage can out for us. _____
3 They just moved into a new flat near the city centre. _____
4 I need your ZIP code to send the package. _____
5 We're planning a vacation to Florida this summer. _____
6 The kids were playing on the sidewalk after school. _____
7 The traffic lights were stuck on red for ages. _____
8 There was a crash at the intersection this morning. _____
9 We ran out of petrol just outside the city. _____
10 There were hundreds of lorries on the motorway on the way here. _____

Practice test

On pages 90–99 you will find an example of what the IELTS Reading exam looks like. Taking this practice test under timed conditions will give you an idea of what it will be like to take the actual exam.

You have one hour to complete the exam. In the paper-based test, this includes the time required to write your answers on an answer sheet. There are three passages, so aim to spend about twenty minutes on each of them.

 Exam tips

Read the instructions carefully. They may be similar to what you have practised before, but maybe not exactly the same.

Read the first task before you start to read each passage so you know how to approach it.

Skip any questions you are not sure about, rather than wasting too much time on a particular question. You can come back to the missing answers later.

Remember to answer all the questions using information from the passages. Whether or not you are knowledgeable about the topic should not make any difference to your answers.

Do not leave answers blank if you run out of time: guess the answers where you can, as there is a chance you will get some right. This is especially true for multiple-choice questions, matching exercises and other questions where you have limited answer options.

READING PASSAGE 1

You should spend about 20 minutes on questions 1–14 which are based on Reading passage 1 below.

The Changing Landscape of Retail

Take a walk through any major shopping district in a large city, and you may notice a shift in what retail spaces are used for. Traditional stores are closing or downsizing and signs advertising vacant units are becoming more common. This change is driven by several factors, including the rise of e-commerce, changing consumer expectations and economic pressures on both businesses and shoppers.

Retail is no longer just about purchasing goods – it is increasingly about the experience. Many consumers now shop online for convenience, price comparison and home delivery. As a result, physical stores are adapting by offering something that online platforms cannot: in-person experiences. These include interactive displays, product demonstrations and personalized customer service. In some cases, stores are becoming more like showrooms, where customers can try products before ordering them online.

Another growing trend is 'destination shopping'. This refers to retail areas designed to attract visitors not just for shopping, but for leisure and entertainment. These spaces often include cafés, restaurants, live events and pop-up shops. The goal is to create a social environment where people want to spend time, even if they do not make a purchase. In cities like Seoul, Singapore and Los Angeles, shopping centres are being reimagined as lifestyle hubs, blending retail with culture and community.

Independent retailers often face greater challenges than large chains, which benefit from bulk purchasing and stronger supply chains. As a result, small businesses may struggle to compete on price or visibility. However, some are finding success by focusing on specialized markets, local products or unique in-store experiences that cannot be replicated online.

Vacant retail spaces are being repurposed in creative ways. In some cities, they are used for temporary exhibitions, seasonal markets or community events. This not only helps fill empty storefronts but also keeps commercial areas vibrant and attractive to visitors. In tourist-heavy destinations such as Kyoto or Dubai, maintaining an appealing retail environment is essential for the local economy.

Another concern is the growing similarity between city centres. As global brands expand, many shopping streets begin to look alike, with the same chain stores appearing in different countries. This phenomenon, sometimes referred to as 'clone towns', can reduce the unique character of a place and make it harder for independent businesses to stand out. In response, some cities are encouraging local entrepreneurship and offering incentives to small retailers to preserve cultural identity.

Service-based businesses – such as salons, fitness studios and cafés – are proving more resilient. These offer experiences that cannot be digitized, and they often benefit from foot traffic generated by nearby shops. As one observer noted, 'You can't have your hair cut online', which helps explain the rise in personal care and hospitality venues in urban centres.

Meanwhile, large retail chains and supermarkets continue to expand on the outskirts of cities, offering convenience and competitive pricing. In many countries, a significant portion of consumer spending now takes place in these locations, further reshaping the role of traditional shopping streets.

QUESTIONS 1–6

Do the following statements agree with the views of the writer? Write:

YES	if the statement agrees with the views of the writer
NO	if the statement contradicts what the writer thinks
NOT GIVEN	if it is impossible to know what the writer's point of view is

1. Online shopping has contributed to the increase in shop closures. _____.
2. Consumers have less money to spend, and this is one reason why traditional stores are not doing well. _____
3. Retail is not about buying things anymore. _____
4. Traditional shops can offer more than online shops can in certain respects. _____
5. Empty shops have been used for performances in some places. _____
6. The expansion of big brands can also make small companies get more noticed. _____

QUESTIONS 7–10

Look at the following features (7–10) and the list of groups below. Match each item with the correct group (A–E).

NB You may use any letter more than once.

7. their changing preferences have caused a major change _____
8. they are becoming more social _____
9. price-based competition is becoming harder for them _____
10. they may get financial help _____

This is true for:

A consumers
B shopping centres
C e-commerce businesses
D independent businesses
E large chains

QUESTIONS 11–14

Choose the appropriate letters a–d to finish sentences 11–14.

11 City centres _____
   a are looking more attractive.
   b attract more independent shops.
   c are losing their distinctive feel.
   d are using more digital technology.

12 Personal care venues are an example of _____
   a businesses that offer services.
   b businesses that are using more digital technology.
   c easily accessible spaces.
   d hair salons.

13 Supermarkets _____
   a are getting bigger in rural areas.
   b have many competitors.
   c have now become larger retail chains.
   d do well outside of city centres.

14 High streets are affected by the growth of physical stores elsewhere, which has _____
   a changed their traditions.
   b changed their pricing.
   c changed their purpose.
   d changed their location.

READING PASSAGE 2

You should spend about 20 minutes on questions 15–27 which are based on Reading passage 2 below.

London's cycle hire scheme

A

Urban transport systems around the world are under increasing pressure. As cities grow in population and complexity, there is a more urgent demand for efficient, sustainable and inclusive mobility solutions. From traffic congestion to air pollution, the challenges are diverse and interconnected. This chapter will explore key transport issues in major cities, with examples from across the globe.

B

One of the most visible problems in large cities is traffic congestion. In cities like São Paulo, Jakarta and Los Angeles, long commute times and gridlocked roads are part of daily life. Congestion not only reduces productivity but also contributes to higher emissions and stress levels. Public transport systems often struggle to keep up with demand. In Mumbai, for example, suburban trains carry more than twice their intended capacity during peak hours, leading to overcrowding and safety concerns.

C

Investing in public transport is a common strategy to reduce car dependency. Cities such as Seoul and Singapore have developed extensive metro and bus networks that are efficient, affordable and widely used. However, building and maintaining such systems requires significant financial and political commitment. In Mexico City, despite a large metro system, many residents still rely on informal minibuses due to gaps in coverage and reliability. Integration between different modes of transport remains a challenge in many urban areas.

D

In response to environmental concerns and the need for healthier transport options, many cities have introduced public bicycle-hire schemes. These systems allow users to rent bikes for short trips, often using mobile apps and docking stations. Paris's Vélib' was one of the first large-scale examples and has inspired similar programs worldwide. New York's Citi Bike, Barcelona's Bicing, and Taipei's YouBike have all seen widespread adoption.

Bike hire schemes offer a flexible and low-emission alternative to motorized transport, especially for short urban journeys. However, they also face challenges such as theft, vandalism and the need for regular maintenance. In some cities, the lack of dedicated cycling infrastructure limits their effectiveness and safety. However, where they are integrated well with public transport and supported by bike lanes, these schemes can significantly enhance urban mobility.

E

Electric scooters (e-scooters) have rapidly emerged as a popular form of micro-mobility in cities such as San Francisco, Berlin and Tel Aviv. They are often used for the 'last mile' of a journey – bridging the gap between public transport stops and final destinations. E-scooters are typically accessed via smartphone apps and can be picked up and dropped off almost anywhere.

While they offer convenience and reduce reliance on cars, e-scooters have also sparked controversy. In many cities, they have been criticized for cluttering sidewalks, causing accidents and operating in legal grey areas. Paris, for instance, recently voted to ban rental e-scooters due to safety concerns. Effective regulation, designated parking zones and public education are essential to ensure that e-scooters contribute positively to urban transport systems.

F

Transport is a major contributor to urban air pollution and greenhouse gas emissions. Cities like Beijing and Delhi have experienced severe air quality crises, partly due to vehicle emissions. Transitioning to electric cars, expanding public transport and promoting active travel (walking and cycling) are key strategies for reducing environmental harm.

Transport systems also have social implications. In many cities, low-income residents live far from job centres and rely on long, expensive commutes. It is clear that ensuring access to affordable and reliable transport is crucial for social inclusion and economic opportunity.

G

The future of urban transport will likely involve a mix of traditional and emerging solutions. Smart technologies, such as real-time data and Artificial Intelligence (AI)-driven traffic management, are already being tested in cities like Singapore and Dubai. However, no single solution fits all contexts. Each city must balance innovation with local needs, infrastructure and culture.

QUESTIONS 15–17

Choose one of the endings (1–7) from the list of endings to complete each sentence below. The information in the completed sentences should accurately reflect what is said in the text.

NB There are more endings (1–7) than sentence beginnings, so you will not need to use them all. You may use each ending once only.

15 A metro or bus system ___ .

16 The introduction of the e-scooter ___ .

17 Air pollution ___ .

List of endings

1 operates on battery power
2 is an urban problem both indoors and outdoors
3 can be costly to set up and run
4 is a significant global problem related to transport
5 influences urban planning
6 has had mixed reactions
7 can help reduce road traffic accidents

QUESTIONS 18–23

Reading passage 2 has an introduction (A) and six other sections B–G.

Choose the most suitable headings for sections B–G from the list of headings below. Write the appropriate numbers (1–11) next to the sections.

NB There are more headings than sections, so you will not use them all.

List of headings
1   Public transport and demand
2   The impact of transport: health, society and environment
3   Alternatives to cars: the need to promote walking, cycling and public transport
4   Congestion and its impact
5   The advantage of metro systems
6   E-scooters: the need for education
7   The rise and reach of bike-sharing programmes
8   Bicycle hire schemes: a flexible and environmentally friendly solution
9   E-scooters: solution or problem?
10 Building better transport: opportunities and obstacles
11 What next? Challenges and innovations

18 Section B _____
19 Section C _____
20 Section D _____
21 Section E _____
22 Section F _____
23 Section G _____

QUESTIONS 24–27

Complete the summary below, each time with ONE WORD from Reading passage 2.

Urban transport systems face growing (24) _____ due to rising populations, congestion and environmental concerns. Cities are investing in public transport, bike hire schemes and (25) _____ to reduce (26) _____ use and emissions. However, issues like overcrowding, safety and inequality persist. Future (27) _____ may include smart technologies, but success depends on local needs, infrastructure and culture.

READING PASSAGE 3

You should spend about 20 minutes on questions 28–40 which are based on Reading passage 3 below.

Personalized exercise

A At the start of every new year, many of us promise ourselves that a certain number of times a week we will go to the gym, go jogging, attend an exercise class, etc. But many of us struggle to fit exercise into our lives, or we start off well and then give up.

B The key could be to find the right type of exercise for you. After all, if we end up doing something we enjoy and can see the benefits of, we are more likely to carry on for longer than a few weeks. Studies suggest that six weeks are all it takes to form a habit, so once we have managed to continue for that length of time, chances are that exercise has become a routine part of our lives that we do not question. So what exercise is right for you? Read on to find out.

C First of all, you need to determine your motivation. Are you mainly interested in de-stressing or in getting fitter? If your ultimate goal is relaxation, then ask yourself if you want to do this energetically, in which case a type of martial art or exercise based on boxing may be right for you. If you have a calmer style, then you could choose solitary exercise, such as walking the dog, doing some gardening, or opting for a brisk daily walk around the block. If you get more motivated from working with others, then you could join a yoga, pilates or t'ai chi class, all designed to stretch and strengthen your muscles and with the added benefit of calming the mind.

D If it is fitness and weight loss you are after, then group activities include military fitness, typically organized in local parks, walking and running groups, dance classes (try line dancing, tap dancing or ballet). Contact your local council for details of those. On your own, you could go horse riding, swimming, or if you fear that you will choose not to leave your house, download fitness and motivational exercise programmes that you can do at home.

E Finally, even people who are incredibly busy have no excuse. It is getting easier to fit exercise into our lives, rather than having to make so many changes to our lifestyles that we are doomed to fail. If you have particular time slots available, then you could book some time with a personal trainer at the weekend who can come to your house, or you could meet them at the gym. During the week, you could use the daily commute for your exercise, by walking faster, parking further away from work, or getting your bicycle out. If you have a more irregular schedule than that, you could choose the next couple of minutes you have spare to try online exercise, or get the skipping ropes out and do some skipping. You could also go outdoors to your nearest fitness trail, or put your running shoes on and run for any length of time, as everything counts when you are doing exercise.

F You see? There is no excuse. Whatever your lifestyle, you will be able to find something that suits you. Just sit down with a cup of tea, read this article again, have a think about your options. Then finish the tea, get up, get going, and don't stop.

QUESTIONS 28–33

Use NO MORE THAN THREE WORDS from the passage to complete each blank in the diagram below.

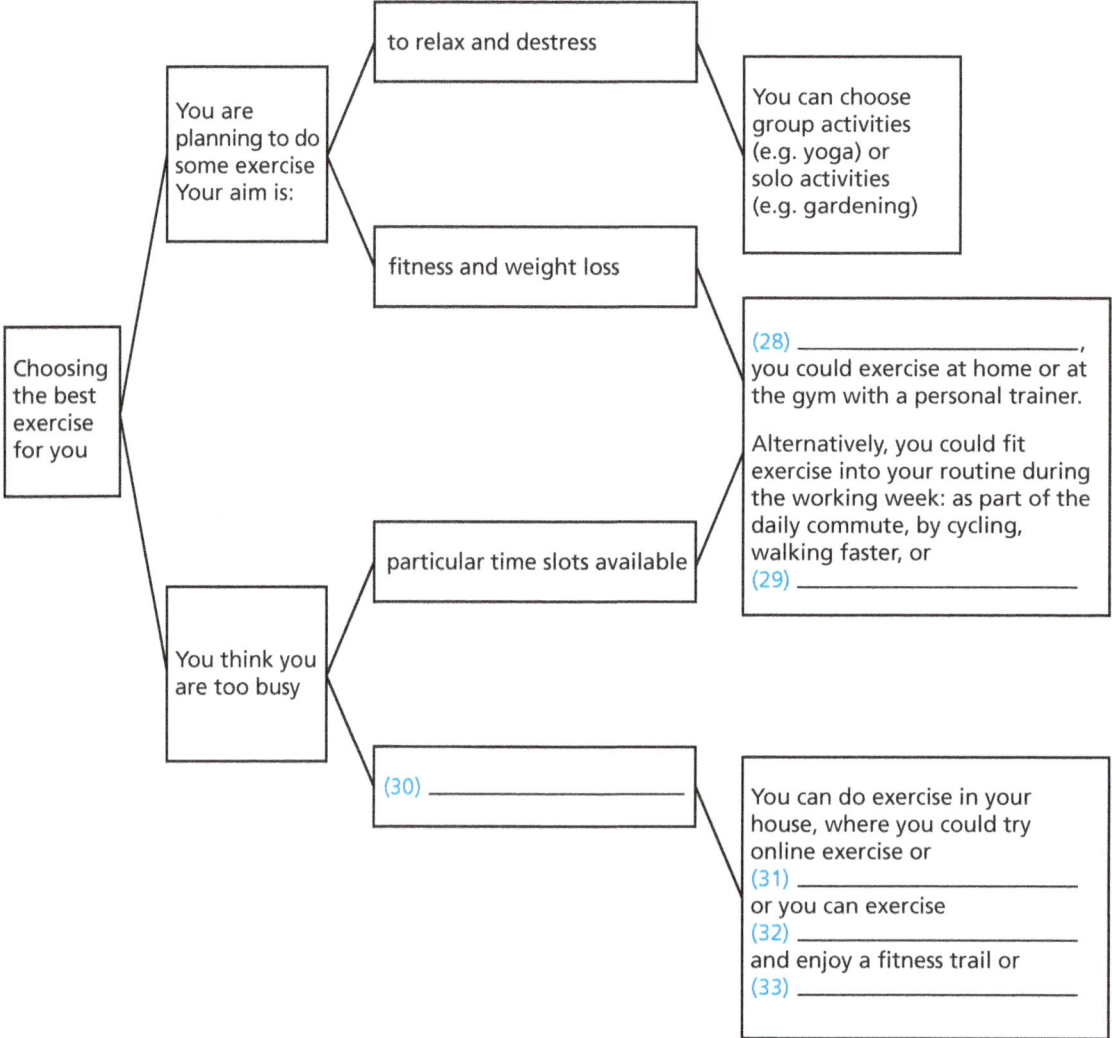

QUESTIONS 34–36

Reading passage 3 has six paragraphs A–F. Which paragraphs state the following information? Write the appropriate letters A–F next to numbers 34–36.

NB There are more paragraphs than summaries, so you will not use them all.

34 It is recommended to take action without delay. _____
35 Suitable exercise will be more long term. _____
36 Choose your exercise depending on your purpose. _____

QUESTIONS 37–38

Using NO MORE THAN THREE WORDS from the text for each, answer the following questions.

37 How can activities such as walking and gardening be described?
_____

38 Who can provide information about organized sports or fitness activities with others?
_____

QUESTIONS 39–40

Do the following statements agree with the information in the passage? Write:

TRUE	if the text confirms the statement
FALSE	if the text contradicts of the statement
NOT GIVEN	if it is impossible to know from the text

39 It is important to try and exercise for six weeks without giving up. _____
40 Having a cup of tea is part of a healthy lifestyle. _____

Answer key

Unit 1 Friendship

Part 1 Vocabulary

Exercise 1a
2 sharing
3 having fun
4 chatting

Exercise 1b
1 sharing
2 Partying
3 Chatting
4 having fun

Exercise 2
1 basketball
2 yoga
3 dancing
4 board games

Exercise 3a

Jack, 15: I spend time with my family most evenings. At the weekend, I prefer to hang out with my friends at the park or in the playground in the local woods. If it rains, I like to go to see a film with my friends.

Monica, 18: I go to a chess club which meets twice a month, and once a year we go camping. It's the highlight of my summer! We stay in tents on a lovely camp site and have picnics and barbecues. In the evenings, we organize quizzes and play cards. And we also play a lot of chess, of course!

Amrita, 12: My older sisters spend a lot of time with their friends in the local shopping centre, but I'm not allowed to go out without an adult yet. I can still chat to my friends a lot after school though, but I go online to do that.

Exercise 3b
1 shopping centre
2 an adult
3 a camp site
4 a picnic

5 barbecues (singular: a barbecue)
6 quizzes (singular: a quiz)

Part 2 Skills development

Exercise 3
Suggested answers:
1 Why are Ben, Rory and Carlos mentioned in the article?
2 Which of the following best describes Ben?
3 What do we know about the lake that Rory visits?
4 Carlos mentions that he is left-handed because …
5 The answers to the recent research and the answers from the readers…

Exercise 4
1 The correct answer is b – It is true what is said in d: they are teenage boys, but they are mentioned because what they said about themselves is part of the article (b). c says that they read magazines, but we only know that they are readers of the magazine that the text was in, not that they read magazines in general, and in any case this would not be enough of a reason for them to appear in this magazine. a is not correct: they say why *they* value friendship, but we don't know if this is true about all teenagers.

2 The correct answer is d – we know he likes football and skateboarding. It is true that he has fights with his parents sometimes (a), but we don't know that he often fights, or that he fights with other people. b says that he generally likes to be alone, but we only know that that is true after he has had a fight with his parents. We have no information about c because we don't know how happy he and his friends are.

3 The correct answer is b – when people say something is nearby, without saying near what, they mean near their house. It may be in a village (d) or near the school (a) too, but we cannot be sure. As Rory uses the lake for water sports, it is likely that other people do too, but the text does not tell us that *a lot of* people do (c).

4 The correct answer is b – we have no information about a or d. It may be an interesting fact (c) but there is a reason why he mentions it: his friends had to copy his notes for him. This is because he is left-handed and

uses his left hand for writing: being left-handed made the situation more difficult for him (b).

5 The correct answer is c – a is incorrect: the article says the results were not really surprising. Although sports were mentioned, d is incorrect because the results were about what teenagers say is important to them. The results were not exactly the same (b), but they were similar (c) because some aspects of them were the same: the research said that *they value friendship above everything else*; the readers said that *they value friendship very highly*.

6 d
d is the correct answer as the text refers to strangers where it says *people who in the future may become our friends*. We could say that a is true and b is false, as the definition of 'stranger' is *a person we have not met before*. However, this is not mentioned in the text. c is often said, but again there is no evidence of this in the text. It is important that your answer reflects what is said in the text, so don't rely on your general knowledge or opinion.

Part 3 Exam practice

1 a
30 or fewer (a) is the same as *no more than 30*, and (b) means 30 friends or more; in (c) 400 refers to friends over the whole of people's lives, whereas *at any particular point* means at any given time (as in (a)). The number in (d) is about online friends, for which there was actually a range from 150 to 180.

2 d
Friendship means different things in different situations (the end of the first paragraph) means that a definition of friendship is difficult: it depends on the situation. The other items are not correct. The following are mentioned: *the numbers* (a), *keeping friends* (not: keeping them *happy* (b)) and *social media* (c). However, the specific statements are not true.

3 a
Paragraph 3 describes different views that people have about friendship and therefore says that it means different things to different people (a). The other options are views that people may have but the text does not say that those are what friendship means.

4 c
In the text, *we fear we have left it too late in life to start*, corresponds to *they worry because they think they are too old*. b is not mentioned. People may have many friends (a) but this is not something that is described as a worry. d is true, and it may lead to problems, but again, this is not described as something that people worry about.

5 d
Something that is *shared by many* is something that people have in common. Here this refers to *the need to be around other people* (d). The dissatisfaction refers to the different meanings of friendship, not to friends themselves (a). b and c may be true, but there is no evidence of that in the text.

Unit 2   Body and mind

Part 1   Vocabulary

Exercise 1a
1 fitness
2 diet
3 illness
4 age

Exercise 1b

Diet	Fitness	Age	Illness
fruit	exercise	adult	disease
nutrition	gym	ageing	injury
nuts	sport	teenager	medicine
vegetables	training	youth	medical condition

Exercise 2a
positive feelings: amazed, confident, curious, relaxed
negative feelings: angry, annoyed, bored, depressed, disappointed, embarrassed, guilty, jealous, nervous, tired

Exercise 2b

amazement	amazed
anger	angry
annoyance	annoyed
boredom	bored
confidence	confident
curiosity	curious
depression	depressed
disappointment	disappointed
embarrassment	embarrassed
guilt	guilty
jealousy	jealous
nervousness	nervous
relaxation	relaxed
tiredness	tired

Exercise 2c
1 Anger
2 embarrassment
3 Boredom
4 Depression
5 tiredness
6 Relaxation
7 amazement

Part 2   Skills development

Exercise 1
1 nine
2 ten
3 eleven
4 thirteen

Exercise 2
1 The student used three words. As the maximum is two words and/or a number, correct answers include *the 2020s (two words), the twenty-twenties (two words), 2020s (one word), twenty-twenties (one word), twenties (one word), the twenties (two words)*.
2 The student used three words: COVID-19 has a hyphen in it which counts as one word. Correct answers would be *COVID-19 (one word), COVID-19 pandemic (two words)*.
3 The student used two words. This answer is correct.
4 This answer needs to be shortened. The correct answer would be *global monitoring* as this answers 'how'.

Exercise 3
Possible answers:
1 regular exercise (2 words)
2 I love it (3 words)
3 reading, watching films (3 words)
4 to keep fit (3 words)

Exercise 4
The following wouldn't help:
reading the text before reading the questions; identifying the key words in the text.

Exercise 5
Suggested answers:
1 <u>What</u> does the <u>younger</u> generation usually think <u>health means</u>?
2 To <u>feel healthy</u>, what do <u>older</u> people feel they still need to be <u>able to do</u>?
3 <u>Who</u> could <u>benefit</u> from the <u>survey</u>?

Exercise 6
Suggested answers:
1 physical fitness
2 everyday tasks
3 health professionals

Part 3 Exam practice

Questions 1–6
1 poorer people
2 correct answers: mental, mental health, mental illness
3 rich societies
4 correct answers: men, middle-aged men
5 age, height
6 correct answers: appearance, their appearance

Questions 7–8
7 c
8 a

Unit 3 Studying abroad

Part 1 Vocabulary

Exercise 1a
1 c
2 d
3 a
4 b

Exercise 1b
1 geography
2 numeracy
3 history
4 literacy

Exercise 2
1 nursery school
2 primary school
3 secondary school
4 bachelor's degree
5 master's degree
6 PhD

Exercise 3
1 Vietnam
2 Hanoi
3 Japan
4 Kyoto
5 Arabic
6 Egyptian
7 Cairo
8 German
9 Heidelberg
10 Dutch
11 Maastricht
12 Dutch
13 Brussels
14 German
15 Zurich

Exercise 4
1 English
2 French
3 Vietnamese
4 Japanese
5 Swiss
6 German
7 Dutch
8 Belgian

Part 2   Skills development

Exercise 1
Paragraph numbers 2 and 3 (under 'The benefits of studying abroad')

Exercise 2

Countries	People	Institutions or departments
Australia the UK the US Germany China Malaysia Japan Russia Nigeria Brazil the Netherlands India	Russell Howe Manal	Stellinga International College the faculty of Art and design (at Stellinga)

(note: Europe is not a country)

Exercise 3

numbers	10, one, two, 5, 11th, 1
words in italics	needed, wanted internationalization
words in bold print	[the title and all subheadings]
abbreviations	UK, US, i.e., e.g.

Exercises 4 and 5
1 paragraphs 2 and 3 – the quotation marks help to find this answer.
2 that it was a choice (something he wanted to do), and not a necessity (something he needed to do). The italics make it clear that he wants to emphasize this.
3 the first and last paragraph – in the first paragraph, it mentions 'most welcoming' and talks about Germany as the country at the top of the list. In paragraph 4, the uppercase letter G of Germany is easy to spot and the word 'winner' appears very near.
4 paragraph 4 – internationalization is printed in italics.

Part 3   Exam practice
Suggested answers:
1 equivalent
2 International Baccalaureate
3 personal statement
4 1000 words
5 passport
6 A
7 F
8 B
9 D

Review 1

Exercise 1
There are, of course, different possibilities, but here are some examples of right and wrong answers. Notice how some of the ones on the left are like sentences, whereas the ones on the right use more nouns and are like titles.

	wrong (too long)	right
1	chicken, rice and peas	chicken and rice
2	I went to work	office work
3	meeting my wonderful wife	meeting my wife
4	do what you think is best for you	follow your dreams
5	travelling around the whole world on a luxury boat	a world cruise
6	getting a high enough IELTS score to study in the UK	passing IELTS *OR* studying abroad

Exercise 2
1 j – You can spend time and you can spend money (see f), but sentence f does not match grammatically.
2 k
3 h
4 a – You could also live near the woods (see i) but you wouldn't just live there in your spare time.
5 d
6 c
7 f – Sentence ending e is not correct because of the extra 'that'.
8 g – You can play sports and musical instruments (see h), but sentence h does not match grammatically. Adults do not 'play' with their friends (see l).

Exercise 3
1 charge fees
2 take a class
3 keep in touch
4 have fun
5 value friendship
6 play cards
7 study abroad

Exercise 4
Suggested answers:
1 When I have no college work, I usually go to my friends to play cards / computer games / sports. / When I have no college work, I usually go and spend time with my friends.
2 Partying with friends is my favourite activity.
3 There is no need to be embarrassed, just come in. [correct]
4 To my amazement, she had prepared a picnic.
5 Depression is a common medical condition.
6 His worst injury (after his accident) was a broken arm. / His worst disease (in his lifetime) was COVID-19.
7 He does a lot of yoga. / He plays a lot of basketball.
8 I have been feeling very tired.

Exercise 5
Possible answers:
1 bored, tired
2 depressed, disappointed, bored, annoyed, tired
3 annoyed, angry
4 confident
5 relaxed, tired

Exercise 6
1 literacy
2 numeracy
3 student
4 university
5 degree
6 research
7 diploma
8 application

Unit 4 Science and technology at home

Part 1 Vocabulary

Exercise 1a
2 gas
3 liquid
4 solid

Exercise 1b
1 states of matter
2 liquid
3 solid
4 gas

Exercise 2a
2 a
3 h
4 b
5 f
6 c
7 e
8 j
9 d
10 i

Exercise 2b
Suggested answers:
1 *a biography*: a book / story about another person's life
2 *an autobiography*: a book you write about yourself / written by the author about their own life

Part 2 Skills development

Exercise 1
1 d
2 a
3 b
4 c
5 f
6 e

Exercise 2
1 d
2 a
3 e
4 c
5 f
6 b

Exercise 3
2 There are some materials that allow electricity to pass through them. These electrical conductors are used in many different appliances in the home.
3 Another example is electrical insulators, substances that do not let electricity pass through.
4 Your smartphone's operating system may be the same or a different underline{OS} to the one controlling your tablet.

Exercise 4

Mobile phone components *[1 parts]*
An average *[2 typical]* basic mobile phone contains a circuit board, an antenna, a liquid crystal display, a keyboard, a microphone, a speaker and a battery.

Mobile metals
Mobiles contain *[3 include]* different metals:

- Copper is used for electrical circuits because it is a good electrical conductor.
- Silver is used in switches on the circuit boards and in the phone buttons because it is an even better electrical conductor. It lasts for millions *[4 a very large amount]* of on/off cycles.
- Gold is used to plate the surfaces of the circuit board and the connectors. It is an excellent *[5 exceptional]* electrical conductor and does not corrode.
- Tantalum is used in the electronic components. It enables scientists to make mobiles very small *[6 tiny]*.

Your mobile is also likely to contain palladium, platinum, aluminium and iron.

Electrical conductivity
Metals conduct *[7 transfer]* electrical currents well. Non-metals usually make good insulators. In a mobile, electrical insulators surround the circuit

Smart mobiles
The next *[8 following]* generation of mobile could be made from 'smart' fabric *[9 material]*. These types of fabric react to something in the environment and change. A smart fabric mobile could be folded and put in your pocket without breaking.

Part 3 Exam practice
Questions 1–4
1   chemical reaction
2   separated (out)
3   refuse
4   source

Questions 5–7
5   chemically synthesized compounds
6   contaminated sources
7   artificial flavours

Unit 5   Back to nature
Part 1   Vocabulary
Exercise 1
1   waterfall
2   valley
3   bay
4   cliff

Exercise 2
1   dune
2   desert
3   meadow
4   cave

Exercise 3a
The words that refer to the natural world are underlined below. :

Our knowledge of natural history would not be what it is today without the work of women explorers, artists and scientists. In this leaflet, you will learn about three British pioneering women, first to be involved in uncovering some of the rich history of the natural world.

Mary Anning (1799–1847)
Mary came from a poor family who lived in Lyme Regis, a coastal town in the South West of England. Her father tried to make extra money by selling fossils (remains in rocks) to rich tourists. Consequently, Mary and her siblings learned from an early age how to look for fossils, although she was the only one of the brothers and sisters who became an expert because she understood that fossils were of interest to geology and biology, not just tourism. However, in her lifetime she did not always get the credit she deserved, as it was male geologists who published the descriptions of any finds. Her important finds include the first skeleton of an ichthyosaur, or fish-lizard, a plesiosaur, also known as sea-dragon, and a pterodactyl, a 'flying dragon'.

Collecting fossils on the cliffs was dangerous work. Mary's dog Tray was killed when rocks and earth fell down a cliff, and she nearly lost her life in the same landslide, but in the end it was cancer that killed her when she was 47.

Dorothea Bate (1878–1951)
Born in the Welsh countryside, she had a passion for outdoor pursuits and natural history from an early age. She became the first female scientist in the Natural History museum in London. She was a palaeontologist, that is, a scientist who studies fossils in order to understand the history of life on Earth. She went to mountains and cliffs in the Mediterranean and explored hilltops in Bethlehem, discovering and documenting animal fossils. She wrote hundreds of reports, reviews and papers.

Evelyn Cheesman (1881–1969)
Although Evelyn wanted to become a veterinary surgeon, this was not possible for women in the early twentieth century. Instead, she trained as a canine nurse. Her first job, however, was not related to dogs: she worked in the insect house at the London Zoological society. She was very adventurous and went on many expeditions to remote locations, as far away as the Galapagos Islands. Despite being very busy, she managed to publish 16 books.

Exercise 3b
Lyme Regis – a coastal town in the South West of England

fossils – remains in rocks

siblings – brothers and sisters

ichthyosaur – fish-lizard

plesiosaur – sea-dragon

pterodactyl – flying dragon

Tray – Mary's dog

landslide – rocks and earth [falling] down a cliff

palaeontologist – scientist who studies fossils in order to understand the history of life on Earth

canine – related to dogs

remote – far away

Exercise 4a
The linking words are highlighted in the text (see Exercise 3a above).

Exercise 4b
1 d
2 a
3 f
4 b
5 c
6 e

Part 2 Skills development

Exercise 2
(Compare your drawing to the diagrams in exercise 3 to see if you included the main aspects.)

Exercise 3
1 mud, sand or soil
2 deeper (and deeper)
3 rock
4 (start to) crystallize
5 process
6 waves, tides and currents
7 break off

Part 3 Exam practice

1 drumsticks
2 (green) pods
3 green beans
4 nutrients
5 pickled/dried
6 dried/pickled
7 spinach
8 skin infections
9 joints
10 digestion
11 pleasant
12 milk flow
13 delicacy

Unit 6 Communication

Part 1 Vocabulary

Exercise 1
1 slogan
2 sign
3 logo
4 advertisement

Exercise 2a
Suggested answers:

It's impossible to avoid <u>advertisements</u>. In our homes, <u>newspaper</u>, <u>magazine</u>, <u>television and online ads</u> compete for our attention. <u>Posters</u>, <u>billboards</u> and <u>flyers</u> greet us the moment we walk out the door. Advertising agencies stay busy thinking up new ways to get our attention. We have company <u>logos</u> on our clothes. Our <u>email</u> is full of <u>spam</u>, and <u>pop-ups</u> slow us down when we read <u>articles</u> on our <u>social media feeds</u>. <u>Product placement</u> sneaks into <u>films</u> and <u>TV shows</u>. On free <u>streaming channels</u> we are unable to skip the <u>TV commercials</u>. Advertisers have also tried to advertise in a subliminal way (influencing viewers' minds without them knowing it), e.g. by using colour, shapes or sounds in <u>ads</u> to strengthen brand awareness. It's no wonder that this is called the consumer age.

1 spam
2 product placement
3 billboards
4 flyers
5 consumer
6 pop-ups

Exercise 2b
2 magazine
3 television
4 online
5 advertising
6 company
7 product
8 TV
9 brand
10 consumer

Exercise 3a
1 audience
2 opinions
3 brands
4 products
5 consumers
6 trust

Exercise 3b
1 A
2 an
3 a
4 the
5 the

Part 2 Skills development

Exercise 1

nouns	verbs	adverbs
satellite	transfer	fast
newspaper	free	cheaply
mobile	signal	
transfer	access	
access		
keyboard		
consumer		
signal		

Exercise 2
2 verb e.g. *return*
3 verb ending in *–ing*, e.g. *communicating*; verb ending in *–ed*, e.g. *communicated*
4 adjective starting with a consonant (if it started with a vowel it should say 'an', not 'a' in front of it). Possible answers are *good* or *clever*. However, as there is a comparison to the past, a comparative form would work well: *better*.
5 adverbs, e.g. *mainly* or *mostly*, and *sometimes* or *increasingly*
6 preposition: *into*

Exercise 3
The notes relate to the first part of the text, and the summary to the last part.

a
<u>types of communication</u>:
1 **spoken**
2 written
3 **non-verbal**

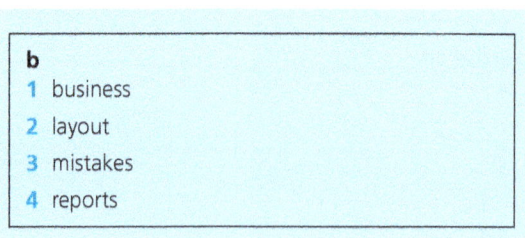

b
1 business
2 layout
3 mistakes
4 reports

Part 3 Exam practice

Questions 1–9
1 participants
2 plan
3 time
4 achieve
5 future
6 necessary
7 effective
8 employees
9 preventing

Questions 10–12
10 communication problems
11 writing skills
12 important elements

Review 2

Exercise 1
Check that you have used a maximum of five words.

Exercise 2
1 Although
2 For example
3 and
4 such as
5 also
6 However

(Note: you cannot start a sentence with *such as*)

Exercise 3
1 b
2 a

Exercise 4
1 a – product placement
2 d – coastal town
3 e – public library
4 f – advertising agency
5 c – natural history
6 g – women explorers
7 b – outdoor pursuits
8 h – veterinary surgeon
9 i – marine animal

Exercise 5
1 fossil
2 seashells
3 jellyfish
4 tracks/footprints

Exercise 6
1 Geology – Biology
2 chronometer – barometer
3 television – mobile phone / smartphone
4 holidays – expeditions
5 bone – water
6 one-way – two-way

110 Reading for IELTS

Unit 7 Business management

Part 1 Vocabulary

Exercise 1
1 b
2 e
3 d
4 a
5 i
6 h
7 g
8 c
9 f

Exercise 2a

Saving money	Borrowing money from the bank	Getting your own money from the bank	Earning money	Paying money
investment	owe	ATM	salary	mortgage
savings account	mortgage	withdrawal	income	rent
	loan	cash point		purchase
	credit card	debit card		fees
				fines
				debit card
				credit card

Exercise 2b
1 cash point or ATM
2 fine
3 fees
4 loan
5 mortgage

Exercise 3
1 a
2 b

Part 2 Skills development

Exercise 1

explanation (x 3)	the companies that are quoted in the leading share price indices
	small and medium-sized enterprises, with less than 250 employees
	90 per cent of all firms
reason (x 3)	they can create economic growth, innovation and new jobs
	its expanding digital economy, young workforce and supportive government schemes
	forcing entrepreneurs to go through planning steps to make sure their business propositions are viable
example	new and developing small businesses
comparison	the numbers have otherwise increased year on year and we now see the best figures ever recorded
condition	if new entrepreneurs are to succeed, if new businesses are to thrive

Exercise 2a and 2b

1 Paragraph A: c – the paragraph starts talking about large companies, and the attention that the media gives them, but this is just background information which serves as a contrast to the important information about small businesses that follows.

The topic sentence is: *However, most economists agree that smaller businesses, particularly new and developing small businesses, are crucial to the long-term success of any economy.*

2 Paragraph D: b – the topic sentence is *India is a particular success story.*

3 Paragraph E: b – the topic sentence is *If new entrepreneurs are to succeed, if new businesses are to thrive, then it is important that they appreciate the central role of planning.*

Exercise 3
1 Which <u>paragraph</u> mentions <u>statistics</u>? B

2 In paragraph <u>A</u>, which <u>word</u> indicates that the text will <u>not</u> be about <u>large businesses</u>?
However

3 In paragraph <u>C</u>, <u>who</u> are said to be the <u>people</u> and/or <u>organizations</u> that can make <u>start-ups happen</u>?
investors and *governments*

4 In paragraph E, which sentences state the benefits of a business plan?

A business plan is the basis of new business development, and it encourages an entrepreneur to think ahead and plan, as far as possible, for the business to be successful.

and

However, it is an invaluable exercise, forcing entrepreneurs to go through planning steps to make sure their business propositions are viable.

Part 3 Exam practice

Questions 1–5
1 B
2 E
3 H
4 F
5 D

Questions 6–8
6 commitment
7 funds
8 accept

Unit 8 Arts and literature

Part 1 Vocabulary

Exercise 1a

visual arts	literary arts	performing arts
photography	poetry	music
painting	non-fiction	directing
jewellery	fiction	dance
interior design		acting
architecture		
sculpture		

Exercise 1b
1 visual arts
2 non-fiction
3 dance
4 directing
5 interior design
6 jewellery

Exercise 1c
1 architecture
2 directing
3 fiction
4 performing arts

Exercise 2
1 the photographs of the people partying on the beach with my sisters
2 the importance of the education I received in the UK
3 the details of the art theft which included the royal items of jewellery
4 the secret of a successful career

Part 2 Skills development

Exercise 1a

Examples of possible answers:

1 preposition (e.g. **in** Egypt, **near** the pyramids)
2 noun (e.g. **history**, **artefacts**)
3 verb (e.g. **to think** about) or preposition (e.g. **into** its galleries)
4 verb (e.g. **is** the website, **should be** consulted)
5 noun (e.g. **drink**)

Exercise 1b

1 c   2 e   3 d   4 a   5 b

Exercise 2

1 **b** – Museums help us interpret our surroundings. ('*they give generations of visitors the opportunity to make sense of the world around them*'; **a** is not mentioned in the text; in **c** 'parties' is wrong, the meaning of 'celebrate' in the text is about giving attention to and honouring art and science)

2 **c** – The increase in tourism makes us consider its ecological impact. ('*this raises questions about sustainability: can the needs of tourists be balanced with environmental concerns?*'; **a**: a period of ten years is mentioned, not more than one decade; the 100,000 in **b** relates to the number of museums, not visitors)

3 **a** – The GEM exemplifies sustainable tourism. ('*world leaders in sustainable tourism … the Grand Egyptian Museum (GEM), is a good case in point*'; **b**: the water is the amount that is saved rather than what is used; **c**: the museum promotes eco-tourism but does not force anyone)

4 **c** – The GEM has a positive influence on nearby businesses. ('*The museum enhances financial sustainability … in the way it attracts international visitors who contribute to the local economy by spending on retail, food and drink, accommodation and transport*; **a**: it collaborates with educational institutions but we do not know about talks in schools specifically; **b**: the text just says that the GEM makes *discussions* about heritage protection easier)

5 **c** – The GEM cares about both the future and the past. ('*the museum aims "to preserve … heritage [the past] while contributing to a more sustainable future for generations to come [the future]"* '; **a**: visitors spend on accommodation and transport, not the museum; **b**: nothing is said here about what the museum shows – the environment, culture and finance are mentioned in relation to sustainability)

Part 3 Exam practice

Questions 1–5

1 F ('*Reading is something which matters to everyone: … it has an emotional, educational impact on people*')

2 E ('*Readers are not passive participants in a story; they engage with the information in books and with the entertainment they bring. (…) By reading about the characters' experiences they will also share their emotions, such as joy, excitement and sadness.*')

3 I ('*It could be argued that a reader's contribution to a story is equal to what the author [= writer] of the text has put into it.*')

4 D ('*Stories like these are part of many traditions around the world, and a record and reminder of the values, traditions and languages of their cultures.*')

5 H ('*More recent evidence of the social importance of stories can be found in book groups, mostly run from people's homes and within their own social circles. Fiction is also discussed all over social media…*')

Questions 6–8

6 impact
7 characters
8 discussed

Unit 9   Community matters

Part 1   Vocabulary

Exercise 1
1 centre
2 policing
3 service
4 care
5 spirit

Exercise 2
communal: c – adjective: belonging or relating to a community as a whole; something that is shared

a commune: b – noun: a group of people who live together and share everything

communally: a – adverb: together; if things are done or happen in this way, they are shared by everyone in a group

Exercise 3

	adjective	verb	adverb	noun
criminal	✓	criminalize (note: we say 'to commit' a crime)	criminally	✓
volunteer	voluntary	✓	voluntarily	✓
loyalty	loyal	(verb: 'to be loyal')	loyally	✓
residential	✓	to reside	residentially (formal)	residence, resident
punish	punished punishable punishing	✓	punishingly	punishment

Exercise 4
1 a – political party
2 f – online community
3 g – voluntary organization
4 b – film cast
5 c – rock band
6 d – friendship group
7 e – sports team

Part 2   Skills development

Exercise 1
1 B
2 C
3 C
4 D, E, F, G
5 functionalist theory, conflict theory, symbolic interactionism theory
6 functionalist theory: paragraphs D and G

Exercise 2
1 C (paragraph E)
2 A (paragraph D)
3 A (paragraph G)
4 A (paragraph D: *discourage isolation and selfishness*)
5 B (paragraph F)

Part 3   Exam practice

Questions 1–6
1 A – last but one paragraph of the text: *Communities, in all their forms, offer both practical support and a feeling of security*

2 E – see section on **Types of Communities**: *These tight-knit communities are often viewed as places where, regardless of material wealth, people feel rich in terms of social bonds, as everyone looks out for one another.* This only mentions feeling rich and does not say how much money people have. Money is also not mentioned elsewhere in the text.

3 A – Paragraph 1: *The concept of 'community' is complex and can be difficult to define precisely.*

4 D – see section on **Types of Communities**: *These meet-up groups are usually set up in response to a need in a particular context.*

5 A – last but one paragraph of the text: *They enable individuals to access resources, gain knowledge and take part in activities that would be difficult to accomplish alone,* and *collective efforts amplify individual power* (see second paragraph in **Common Features of Communities**)

6 C – see section on **Types of Communities**: *What sets these traditional communities apart from others, is that their members are not just emotionally close, but also there in person to help each other.*

Questions 7–8
7 neighbours
8 shallow

Review 3

Exercise 2

global – multinational (paragraph 1)

importance – value (paragraph 1)

develop – evolve (paragraph 1)

supports – underpins (paragraph 2)

help – assist (paragraph 2)

first – initial (paragraph 2)

particularly –especially (paragraph 2)

decline – downturn (paragraph 3)

encourage – promote (paragraph 3)

vital – crucial (paragraph 4)

Exercise 3
1 e
2 c
3 a
4 b
5 d

Exercise 4
Check the text on page 68 for the original sentences. The sentences are likely to be followed by:

1 a noun phrase = (article) (adjective) noun)
2 a verb
3 noun phrase or pronoun
4 a noun phrase
5 -*ing* form
6 *in* and noun
7 comparative adjective (e.g. *better, higher, more important* …)

Exercise 5
1 In my community, there are **a few** problems with graffiti, but not very many.
2 If one of my students has disorganized notes, I know they will have problems revising. (correct – *they* can refer to an individual)
3 I dislike it when I have to use a communal bathroom. (correct)
4 The person who is standing next to my sister is taller than her, but only because they are wearing a hat. (correct – the person is taller than my sister because they are (he or she is) wearing a hat)

Exercise 6
1 rock band
2 sports team
3 community policing

Answer key 115

Unit 10 History

Part 1 Vocabulary

Exercise 1a
Visit a museum, in recent years, a national tradition, a historical document.

Exercise 2a

nouns	adjectives
period	historical
era	former
century	modern
historian	ancient

Exercise 2b
1 ancient
2 period
3 century
4 era
5 former
6 modern

Exercise 3
1 b
2 d
3 a
4 c

Part 2 Skills development

Exercise 1a

A

It is <u>not easy to compare the artistic styles and periods of different countries</u>, especially as they may use different words to refer to the same features, and perhaps occasionally also use the same words with a slightly different meaning. Moreover, particular styles and periods overlap.

Exercise 1b
Suggested answers:

B

An example of this is the <u>'Victorian'</u> period in Britain, which has a style that is often described as romantic. First of all, the name of this period links it immediately with British royal history, which potentially creates <u>confusion</u> to <u>non-British people</u> who <u>may not be aware</u> that the reign of Queen Victoria relates to approximately the <u>second half of the 19th century</u>. Secondly, <u>despite</u> the fact that <u>Queen Victoria died in 1901 the style itself continued into the 20th century</u>. And last but not least, it can be argued that there are <u>distinctly different styles which can all be referred to as Victorian</u>, e.g. the use of flower motifs and pastel colours.

C

<u>Despite</u> Victorian times being characterized by <u>romanticism</u>, the famous British <u>romantic poets belong to the period before Queen Victoria</u>. These are poets such as Robert Burns, William Wordsworth, Samuel Taylor Coleridge and John Keats. From the same era date famous writers such as Jane Austen and Mary Shelley (who wrote Frankenstein), and great architects such as James Wyatt and John Nash. The great painters Gainsborough, Reynolds, Turner and Constable can also be categorized in this period. But who outside of Britain could label this era? And, even if we know they can all be described as <u>Georgian</u> artists, <u>which King George</u> does this refer to? Actually, it refers to <u>four of them</u> (George I, George II, George III and George IV), and thus <u>spans a long period</u> incorporating most of the 18th century and some of the 19th. But <u>then again</u>, there was a <u>Georgian revival</u> in the 20th century, which means the label can also relate to that. Moreover, the style itself <u>incorporates previous styles</u>, including gothic, and has its <u>own subdivision</u>, Regency style, which describes the period of George IV.

D

The period after the Victorian era is referred to as <u>Edwardian</u>, after Edward VII who reigned from 1901 to 1910, when he died. <u>Nobody is sure whether 1910 is the correct end point</u> for the period, with some people suggesting it should be 1912, when the Titanic sank, the start of World War I (1914), its end (1918), or the signing of the post-war peace treaty of Versailles (1919). Elsewhere in Europe, the <u>Art Nouveau era ended around the same time</u>, and unsurprisingly, <u>Art Nouveau</u> is also used to describe the style which was <u>common in Britain</u> at that time. Floral motifs were very common… now where have I heard about that before?

Exercise 1c

first of all (B): introduces the first reason why it is difficult to describe 'Victorian' (you need to be aware of the dates of when British royalty ruled)

secondly (B): gives another reason for the difficulty (the style continued after the end of her reign)

last but not least (B): the last, but also important reason is introduced (different styles could all be referred to as 'Victorian')

despite (C): introduces a contrast (romanticism can refer to Victorian times or the time before)

then again (C): introduces a contrast (Georgian clearly related to the 18th and 19th centuries… but can also refer to the 20th)

moreover (C): another reason for the difficulty in describing what Georgian refers to (it includes previous styles/ and has a subdivision)

unsurprisingly (D): this word indicates that by now the reader will not be surprised to hear that another style (Art Nouveau) is around at the same time as other styles and has elements in common with different styles (e.g. floral motifs, which were also around in Victorian times)

Exercise 1d
B: Victorian, C: Georgian (also mentioned: Georgian revival, gothic, Regency), D: Edwardian (and Art Nouveau)

Exercise 1e
Point d is unsuitable: conclusions should not include new information. The other ideas are very relevant in the conclusion. Point a is essential: the conclusion should pick up the main point. Point b is important as referring back to the main ideas brings the text together. Points c and e emphasize the relevance of the text as they link the issue that is explained in the text to real-life consequences.

Exercise 2

Beaumaris:
a **Beaumaris: a castle of contrasts** (beautiful, but actually military, built fast but not finished). b is incorrect: we know that it is medieval, but we do not know how typical it is. c is incorrect: we know that it is old and Welsh, but we do not know if it is the oldest one.

Edinburgh:
c **Edinburgh Castle and its many roles** – a is incorrect: this question is not really asked or answered, although clearly there is a suggestion that it is a very old castle (*all the way back to* …). b is incorrect: we know that Castle Rock started in the Bronze Age; this means that is has more than 1,000 years of history (from 900 BC to now is over 2,900 years).

Part 3   Exam practice
Questions 1–5
Section A: 2 Law
Section B: 5 Language
Section C: 8 Architecture and Engineering
Section D: 6 Urban Planning
Section E: 4 Religion and Culture

Questions 6–7
6   a
7   c

Unit 11   Crime detection

Part 1   Vocabulary

Exercise 1
1 suspect
2 fingerprint
3 surveillance
4 DNA evidence

Exercise 2a
1 g
2 d
3 b
4 a
5 i
6 f
7 h
8 c
9 e

Exercise 2b
to analyse: the noun is analysis

Exercise 2c
1 witness
2 suspect
3 search
4 arrest
5 report

Exercise 2d
1 on
2 with
3 for
4 for
5 to
6 to

Exercise 3
When a crime has been committed, police go to the crime scene to look for clues. They collect evidence like fingerprints, blood or objects left behind. This is part of forensics, which helps solve the case.

If the evidence shows someone did the crime, the police can prosecute them in court. A lawyer will try to prove the person is guilty. If the court decides the person is guilty, they are convicted and may go to prison. But if there isn't enough proof, the person will be found innocent.

Part 2   Skills development

Exercise 1
1 NOT GIVEN – you may know that this is true, or be able to guess it, but the sentence does not mention that computers were used to date the fingerprints.
2 ✓ – date back thousands of years to the time of the ancient Egyptians
3 NOT GIVEN – he probably is, as he seems to have a French name, and he set up a laboratory in France, but this is not actually stated
4 ✓ – Lyons in France
5 ✓ – we know that it is technically possible in 1990 as the sentence says that it was already possible in the 1980s – we do not need to use our own knowledge about DNA or guess
6 ✓ – somebody who is convicted for murder has been found guilty of murder

Exercise 2
1 TRUE – it is given between brackets
2 NOT GIVEN
3 NOT GIVEN – we only know that they assist lawyers in preparing materials
4 NOT GIVEN – it sounds like it is difficult but that is not necessarily true for everyone and the text does not say this
5 TRUE – the text mentions the 'need for precision'
6 NOT GIVEN – we only know that there are tight deadlines

Exercise 3
Part 1
1 TRUE – *Tokyo ... surveillance cameras are now widely used to ...support law enforcement.*
2 NOT GIVEN – we know it is used in transportation hubs but have no details about which crimes or where exactly they have happened
3 TRUE – *CCTV can also ... by giving citizens a false sense of security and encouraging them to be careless with property and personal safety*

Part 2
4 TRUE – *Seoul ...with real-time monitoring*
5 NOT GIVEN – we know they have raised concerns about who has access to CCTV recordings and how they are stored, but nothing else
6 TRUE – *public demand for safer streets, faster emergency response, and more efficient policing.*

Part 3 Exam practice

Questions 1–6
1 FALSE – they are kept apart, not together
2 TRUE – a police officer will arrive first
3 NOT GIVEN – we know that they try to avoid this from happening but we don't know if it sometimes does
4 FALSE – it is photographed four times (see D1–4: each item is photographed individually twice and as part of the crime scene twice)
5 TRUE
6 NOT GIVEN – there is a suggestion that special procedures may be able to save some burnt evidence but we cannot be sure that this is what 'special procedures' refers to

Questions 7–8
C: Recording the scene
E: Hunting for clues

Unit 12 Travel

Part 1 Vocabulary

Exercise 1
1 crossing
2 traffic lights
3 junction
4 pavement

Exercise 2
1 c
2 a
3 b
4 h
5 f
6 e
7 g
8 i
9 d
10 j

Exercise 3
Possible answers:

itinerary: a plan that outlines where you will travel to and your scheduled activities

excursion: a short trip to a nearby location of interest

destination: the place that you are travelling to

travel documentation: the official documents needed for travel, e.g. passports, visas, travel insurance, booking confirmations

Exercise 4a

expressing probability	expressing opinions	expressing facts
presumably	supposedly	undoubtedly
probably	arguably	evidently
possibly	allegedly	actually
it seems unlikely that	from my point of view	in fact
it is difficult to believe that	as far as I am concerned	it is true that
there is a chance that	I would say that	it is a known fact that

Note that some expressions can express both probability and opinion, e.g. supposedly.

Answer key 119

Exercise 4b
1 presumably, probably, supposedly
2 allegedly
3 arguably
4 undoubtedly, evidently
5 actually

Part 2 Skills development

Exercise 1
1 fact
2 fact
3 fact
4 opinion
5 fact
6 fact
7 opinion

Exercises 2a and 2b

Paragraph 1
1 YES – *Public transport is often praised for being …environmentally friendly* (if people praise it, they are aware of it)
2 YES – *it [public transport] does not always meet the needs of all users* ('not … meet the needs of all users' means that some users do not get the service they need, so cannot be satisfied with what they get)
3 NO – *In rural areas… making private vehicles essential* (this means there are some areas where public transport is not enough)
4 NO – *Encouraging greener travel should not mean ignoring …* (this means that other things should not be forgotten (here specifically the diverse needs of commuters))

Paragraph 2
5 NO – *instead of complaining …*
6 NO – *try to save our environment*
7 YES – *try… campaigning for better bus and train networks and … trams*

Paragraph 3
8 YES – *The world's dependency on fuel is something that should concern us all.*
9 YES – *Here are just some examples of the consequences*

10 YES – *The prices of food … also increase as a direct result of the cost of oil, e.g. … beef*
11 YES – *growing popularity of electric vehicles with consumers* (people buy EVs), *easy to charge at home* (practical benefits), *they reduce oil dependence, produce fewer emissions* (environmental benefits) and *provide a quiet and comfortable ride* (a good driving experience).

Exercise 3
1 NOT GIVEN
2 ✓ – people lose their jobs because they can no longer afford to commute to work
3 ✓ – … rely on their own transport for work, e.g. delivery people
4 NOT GIVEN – only the prices of some foods are related to the price of oil, we know about cotton but not about corn
5 NOT GIVEN – car maintenance (keeping a car in good condition by regularly checking it and repairing it when necessary) is not mentioned.

Part 3 Exam practice

Questions 1–6
1 YES – *popularly known* as the Silk Road
2 NOT GIVEN – this is likely, but not stated in the text
3 YES – *Zhang Qian, the Chinese ambassador-adventurer*
4 NOT GIVEN – this is likely, but we do not know that the person who used the name first also used the road
5 NOT GIVEN – this is likely because of its name, but the text does not say it is the main material
6 YES – examples are given of natural materials, e.g. *gems*; man-made materials, e.g. *glass*, and animals: *livestock* is mentioned

Questions 7–9

Correct:
B
F
G

Incorrect:
A (true but tea is not mentioned in the text), C (the exact location is uncertain), D (trade was taking place before formal recorded trade happened), E (true but not mentioned in the text), H (traders had to go around), I (the last part of the journey, towards Chinese civilization, was 800 miles).

Review 4

Exercise 2
1 historical
2 legal
3 global
4 medical
5 religious
6 tourist
7 electric
8 possible

Exercise 3
1 impressive
2 medieval
3 beautiful
4 symmetrical
5 done
6 proud
7 dominates
8 living
9 mainly
10 visitor
11 expensive
12 excellent

Exercise 4
1 arrested
2 charged
3 searched
4 fined
5 sentenced
6 reported

Exercise 5
1 possibly
2 arguably
3 supposedly

Exercise 6
1 AE: *faucet, color* (BE: tap, colour).
2 AE: *neighbor, garbage can* (BE: neighbour, waste bin / refuse bin).
3 BE: *flat* (AE: apartment).
4 AE: *ZIP code* (BE: postcode)
5 AE: *vacation* (BE: holiday)
6 AE: *sidewalk* (BE: pavement)
7 BE: *traffic lights* (AE: stop lights)
8 AE: *intersection* (BE: junction)
9 BE: *petrol* (AE: gas/gasoline)
10 BE: *lorries, motorway* (AE: trucks, freeway/interstate)

Practice test

Questions 1–6

1 YES – *Traditional stores are closing or downsizing... This change is driven by several factors, including the rise of e-commerce.*

2 YES – *Traditional stores are closing or downsizing... This change is driven by several factors, including ... economic pressures on ... shoppers.*

3 NO – *Retail is no longer just about purchasing goods:* this means that retail is still about purchasing goods but that it now is also about more than that.

4 YES – *Physical stores are adapting by offering something that online platforms cannot: in-person experiences.*

5 NOT GIVEN – *Vacant retail spaces are being repurposed in creative ways. In some cities, they are used for temporary exhibitions, seasonal markets, or community events:* it is possible that these events included performances, but they might refer to other types of events.

6 NO – *As global brands expand, many shopping streets begin to look alike ... . This ... can ...make it harder for independent businesses to stand out:* they are noticed less.

Questions 7–10

7 A – *This change is driven by several factors, including ... consumer expectations.*

8 B – *retail areas ... The goal is to create a social environment where people want to spend time, even if they don't make a purchase.*

9 D – *Independent retailers often face greater challenges than large chains, ... As a result, small businesses may struggle to compete on price or visibility.*

10 D – *In response, some cities are encouraging local entrepreneurship and offering incentives to small retailers ...*

Questions 11–14

11 c – *growing similarity between city centres ... many shopping streets begin to look alike... can reduce the unique character of a place*

12 a – *Service-based businesses ... such as salons ...* . Note that hair salons are an example of personal care venues, not the other way around.

13 d – *(large retails chains and) supermarkets continue to expand on the outskirts of cities ... a significant portion of consumer spending now takes place in these locations*

14 c – *large retail chains and supermarkets* [these are physical stores] *continue to expand on the outskirts of cities ... in these locations ... , further reshaping the role* [=purpose] *of traditional shopping streets* [=high streets].

Questions 15–17

15 3 *building and maintaining such* [metro and bus network] *systems requires significant financial ... commitment.*

16 6 *While they offer ..., e-scooters have also sparked controversy* (see E)

17 4 *Transport is a major contribution to urban air pollution* (see F)

Questions 18–23

18 4 (not 1: demand is not the main topic of the section, congestion is)

19 10 (not 5: this is too narrow, the section focuses more broadly on public transport strategies and challenges, and investment in public transport)

20 7 (not 8: the section also talks about challenges like theft, vandalism and infrastructure gaps)

21 9 (not 6: the section covers both pros and cons)

22	2 (not 3: the section also talks about environmental and social impacts)
23	11

Questions 24–27

24	pressure
25	e-scooters
26	car
27	solutions

Questions 28–33

28	at the weekend
29	parking further / parking further away
30	irregular schedule
31	do some skipping / do skipping
32	outdoors
33	run

Questions 34–36

34	F – the paragraph does suggest having a cup of tea and reading the article again, but these are not long activities and the main message of the paragraph is *get up, get going and don't stop*
35	B – if you do something for six weeks it becomes a habit, so it becomes 'long term', the paragraph also talks about the *right type*, or 'suitable', exercise
36	C – this paragraph talks about motivation, reasons to exercise and goals, and suggests matching the type of exercises to these

Questions 37–38

37	solitary exercise
38	(your) local council

Questions 39–40

39	TRUE – see paragraph B
40	NOT GIVEN – in paragraph F, a cup of tea is suggested, but it is not stated why

Glossary

Key

abbr. = abbreviation
adj. = adjective
adv. = adverb
n. = noun
phrasal v. = phrasal verb
phr. = phrase
v. = verb

Unit 1

adult **n.** – a person who is no longer a child

barbecue **n.** – an outdoor party where people cook and eat food

board game **n.** – an indoor game played on a board, usually with pieces that are moved around it, for example chess

camp site **n.** – a place where you can stay on holiday in a caravan or a tent

cards **n.** – a game played with cards that have pictures and numbers on them

chat **n.** – an informal, friendly conversation

close **adj.** – A close relationship or friendship is one in which you know each other well and like each other a lot.

deep **adj.** – A deep relationship is one in which you have strong feelings for each other.

dissatisfaction **n.** – unhappiness

gadget **n.** – a small machine that does something useful

guidelines **n.** – rules or advice about how to do something

hang out **v.** – to spend time in a particular place or with particular people, usually friends

have something in common **phr.** – to have the same interests or opinions as another person or people

keep in touch **phr.** – to continue to write, phone or visit someone although you do not see them often

leisure **n.** – time when you are not working and you can relax and do things you enjoy

picnic **n.** – a meal you eat outside, usually in a field or forest, or at the beach

possession **n.** – something that you own

quiz **n.** – a game in which you have to answer questions

recent **adj.** – having appeared, happened or been made not long ago

research **n.** – work to collect information on a subject

rules **n.** – instructions, often in writing, telling you what you can and cannot do

share **v.** – to give each person in a group a fair or equal part of something

shopping centre **n.** – a large building that contains a lot of shops

social media platforms **n.** – online platforms that allow people to communicate with their friends and other users and to create online communities

spend time **v.** – to pass time in a specific way, activity, place, etc.

stranger **n.** – any person you do not know

temporary **adj.** – for a limited time, not forever

value **v.** – If you value someone or something, you think that they are important and you appreciate them.

weightlifting **n.** – a sport in which people lift heavy weights

woods **n.** – a large area of trees that are growing closely together

Unit 2

concept **n.** – an idea

cope **v.** – If you cope with a situation or problem, you deal with it successfully.

decade **n.** – a period of ten years

disability **n.** – the condition of being unable to use a part of the body or brain because of a physical or mental injury

genetic **adv.** – biologically given from parents to children

height **n.** – the vertical distance from the bottom of something to the top

huge **adj.** – extremely large

illness **n.** – a disease or sickness

impact upon **v.** – to affect a situation, process or person

implication **n.** – something that is likely to happen as a result of something, a consequence

in terms of – If you talk about something in terms of something, you are specifying from what point of view you are considering it.

income **n.** – money you receive, usually from working or from investments

injury **n.** – physical damage or hurt

issue **n.** – a situation or subject that people are talking about

lead to **v.** – If something leads to a situation or event, it causes it to happen.

likely **adj.** – used to say that something will probably happen

limitation **n.** – If someone has limitations, they can only do some things and not others, or they cannot do something very well.

link (to) **v.** – If one thing is linked to another thing, there is a relationship or connection between them.

lose weight **v.** – to become thinner or less heavy

moreover **conj.** – in addition to what has already been said

neighbourhood **n.** – one of the parts of a town where people live

noticeable **adj.** – Something that is noticeable is easy to see, hear or recognize.

obese **adj.** – extremely fat

poverty **n.** – the condition of being poor and without adequate food, etc.

processed **adj.** – prepared in factories

promote **v.** – to encourage something

range (of) **n.** – a series or number of different items

risk **n.** – the possibility of something bad happening

success **n.** – the achievement of something you have been trying to do (successful adj.)

survey **n.** – a set of questions that you ask a large number of people or organizations

symptom **n.** – something wrong with your body or mind that is a sign of an illness

tend (to) **v.** – to usually do something

valuation **n.** – an opinion that someone has about how much the value of something is, what it is worth

vary **v.** – to be different for different people or situations

wellbeing **n.** – the condition of being contented, healthy or successful

Unit 3

ambitious **adj.** – having a strong desire for success or achievement; wanting power, money, etc.

bachelor's degree **n.** – a university degree awarded for an undergraduate course

benefit **n.** – advantage

broaden **v.** – to make or become broader or wider

Glossary 125

elaborate on **v.** – to add information or detail to something that has been said

engineering **n.** – the profession of designing and constructing engines and machinery or structures such as roads or bridges

enhance **v.** – to improve the quality or value of something

equivalent **adj.** – equal in value, quantity, significance, etc.

fluent **adj.** – able to speak or write a foreign language very well

foreign **adj.** – coming from another country

have (things) in common – to resemble one another in specific ways

law **n.** – a rule or set of rules, enforceable by the courts

like-minded **adj.** – Like-minded people have similar opinions, attitudes, interests, etc.

master's degree **n.** – a university degree for further studies after the first/bachelor's degree

nursery school **n.** – a school for young children, usually from three to five years old

on site **adj.** – done or located at the site of a particular activity, etc.

ongoing **adj.** – happening now and likely to continue

overseas **adv.** – in or to foreign countries

PhD **abbr.** – Doctor of Philosophy, the highest university degree

primary school **n.** – a school for children below the age of 11. It is usually divided into an infant and a junior section

procedure **n.** – a way of doing something, especially an established method

proof **n.** – any evidence that shows that something is true

rank **v.** – to put things in position according to importance, size, etc.

secondary school **n.** – a school for young people, usually between the ages of 11 and 18

submit **v.** – to refer something to someone who will make a decision about it

support **n.** – help and kindness given to someone who is in a difficult situation

translation **n.** – something that is or has been changed into a different language

welcoming **adj.** – friendly, especially with visitors, guests, etc.

Unit 4

add **v.** – to put something with something else

appliance **n.** – a machine or device, especially an electrical one used in the home

atmosphere **n.** – the air surrounding the earth or any other planet

button **n.** – a small object you press to make a machine or device work

circuit board **n.** – a board with electronic connections inside a computer, mobile phone, etc.

connotations **n.** – The connotations of a word or phrase are the ideas or qualities that it makes you think of.

conservation **n.** – the protection or careful use of something so that it lasts for a long time

corrode **v.** – If something corrodes, it is gradually destroyed by a chemical action.

distillation **n.** – the process of evaporating or boiling a liquid and condensing its vapour

fall **v.** – to move downwards

fermentation **n.** – a chemical change in which food or a natural substance produces alcohol

fold **v.** – to bend or be bent double so that one part covers another

guess **v.** – to give an answer or opinion that may not be correct because you do not know enough information *harmful* **adj.** – causing or likely to cause damage

icing **n.** – a sweet substance made from powdered sugar, used for decorating cakes, biscuits, etc.

keyboard **n.** – the set of keys that you press to make a computer, mobile phone, etc. work

liquid crystal display **n.** – a flat-screen display used, for example, in portable computers, mobile phones, etc.

mixture **n.** – a combination of different things

operating system **n.** – the set of software that controls the way a computer system works

refuse (to do something) **v.** – to say you will not do something

replacement **n.** – something that you use instead of something else

rise **v.** – to move upwards

sailor **n.** – a member of a ship's crew

source **n.** – the place or thing that you get something from

surface **n.** – the top or outside part of something

surround **v.** – to be all around something

waste **n.** – the use of something in a way that is not necessary

whatsoever **adv.** – used to emphasize a negative statement

Unit 5

bark **n.** – the hard substance on the trunk of a tree

breastfeed **v.** – to feed a baby with milk from the breast

canine **adj.** – relating to dogs

coastal **adj.** – on the land that is next to the sea

come across **v.** – to meet or find someone or something by accident

crab **n.** – a type of shellfish with ten legs that walks sideways

crystallize **v.** – to become a crystal (= a substance that forms naturally into a regular symmetrical shape)

current **n.** – a strong movement of water in a particular direction

deserve **v.** – If you deserve something, you should have it because of your actions or qualities.

deter **v.** – to discourage or prevent something from happening

forehead **n.** – the part of the face above the eyes and below the hairline

frost **n.** – a thin layer of ice particles that form at night on things outside when it is very cold

garnish **n.** – something that is used to decorate food, e.g. a herb

gelatinous adj. – wet and sticky

ground **adj.** – broken up into very small pieces of powder

gum **n.** – a sticky substance that comes out of some plants

in essence **adv.** (phrase) – used to emphasize that you are talking about the central point or idea of a topic

jellyfish **n.** – a soft, translucent sea animal with an umbrella-shaped body with trailing tentacles that sting

layer **n.** – a thickness of a substance that covers a surface

livestock **n.** – animals such as cattle, sheep and hens that are kept on a farm

marine **adj.** – related to the sea, e.g. the animals and plants that live there

meadow **n.** – a field with grass and flowers growing in it

outdoor pursuits **n.** – activities that you do outside in countryside, such as hill walking, trekking, canoeing, kayaking, rafting, climbing, caving

pickled **adj.** – Pickled food is kept in vinegar or sea water to preserve it.

properties **n.** – the qualities or features that something has

publish **v.** – to produce copies of a book or magazine etc. for distribution and sale

relieve **v.** – to reduce pain, distress, etc.

reputed **adj.** – generally considered to be; alleged

rot **v.** – to decay gradually

shallow **adj.** – measuring only a small distance from the top to the bottom of a liquid, not deep

skeleton **n.** – the set of bones that forms a human or animal body

sting **v.** – If an insect, animal or plant stings you, it makes your skin hurt because a sharp part of it, often covered in poison, is pushed into your skin.

stir-fry **n.** – a Chinese dish made by cooking small pieces of meat and vegetables in very hot oil

stomach complaint **n.** – a pain or medical problem of the stomach

surrounding **adj.** – near or all around a place

swollen **adj.** – If part of your body is swollen, it is larger than normal, usually because of an illness or injury.

thrive **v.** – If a plant thrives, it grows very well.

tide **n.** – the cyclic rise and fall of sea level caused by the gravitational pull of the sun and moon. There are usually two high tides and two low tides in each lunar day.

tolerate **v.** – to accept or allow something, even if you may not like it

treasure trove **n.** – a collection or source of valuable objects

wash up **v.** – If the sea washes something up, it carries an object onto a beach and leaves it there.

Welsh **adj.** – relating to Wales

Unit 6

achieve **v.** – If you achieve a particular aim or effect, you succeed in making it happen.

agenda **n.** – a list of subjects that will be discussed at a meeting

argue **v.** – to give the reasons for your opinion, idea, etc.

carry out **v.** – If you carry out a task, you do it.

clue **n.** – something that helps to solve a problem or unravel a mystery

coach **v.** – to teach people a special skill

cogently **adv.** – If you argue something cogently, you give good and convincing reasons.

conflict **n.** – disagreement and argument

convey **v.** – to communicate a message or information

decode **v.** – to convert a message, text, etc. from code into ordinary language

dispute **n.** – an argument or disagreement

drag on **v.** – You say that an event or process drags on when you disapprove of the fact that it lasts for longer than necessary.

draw out **v.** – to pull out or extract

encourage **v.** – to give someone confidence and make them want to do something

engage in **v.** – to take part in a particular activity, especially one that involves competing or talking to other people

facial **adj.** – of or relating to the face

formal **adj.** – following correct or established official methods or style

forum **n.** – a situation or place in which people exchange ideas and discuss issues

gesture **n.** – a movement that you make with a part of your body to express information

greet **v.** – If something greets you, it is the first thing you notice.

interpersonal **adj.** – involving personal relationships between people

keep records **phr.** – to keep a written account of events or facts

layout **n.** – the way in which something appears or is arranged

pop-up **n.** – a small window containing a menu or advertisement that appears on your computer screen

product placement **n.** – a product placed in a TV show, film or social media post intended to be seen by potential customers. A form of advertising.

role **n.** – the part played by a person in a particular situation

season **n.** – a period of time when something takes place or happens

small talk **n.** – light conversation for social occasions

sneak **v.** – to move quietly and secretly

solve **v.** – to find the explanation for or solution to a mystery, problem, etc.

spam **n.** – emails or messages that are sent to you that you did not ask for

sponsor **v.** – to give money for an event, etc., in return for advertising your company

streaming **n.** – the process of providing media online in real time

summarize **v.** – to give the most important points from a speech, report, etc. in a short and clear way

supplier **n.** – an organization or person that provides goods or a service to others

take for granted **v.** – If you say that someone takes you for granted, you are complaining that they benefit from your help, efforts or presence without showing that they are grateful.

to the point – If something you say or write is to the point, it is relevant and does not include unnecessary details.

trade union official **n.** – a person who works for an organization that represents workers and helps to improve working conditions and wages

trade **v.** – to buy and sell things

turn into **v.** – to change into something different

Unit 7

anxious **adj.** – slightly worried

argue **v.** – to try to prove something by giving reasons

booming **adj.** – growing at a rapid rate

commitment **n.** – determination or enthusiasm to do something

current legislation **n.** – the most recent laws

delegate **v.** – to give duties, powers, etc. to another person

draw on **v.** – to use something such as skills or knowledge

encourage **v.** – to give someone confidence and make them want to do something

ensure **v.** – to make certain or sure; guarantee

entrepreneur **n.** – a person who sets up businesses and business deals

enterprise **n.** – a company or business, often a small one

foster **v.** – to promote the growth or development of something

high-profile **adj.** – attracting a lot of attention or publicity

improvement **n.** – work done on something to make it better

lack **v.** – to not have any or not have enough of something *let go of* **v.** – to stop holding something

long-term **adj.** – lasting, staying or extending over a long time

meet someone's needs **v.** – to provide what someone needs

originate **v.** – to start to exist

paperwork **n.** – work that involves writing reports, dealing with letters, filling in forms, etc.

run (a business) **v.** – to be in charge of; manage

sales leads **n.** – the identity of people interested in buying a product or service, the first stage of a sales process

set up **v.** – to start a new business

step back **v.** – to stop for a moment in order to consider something or look at something in a different way

success **n.** – the achievement of something you have been trying to do

successive **adj.** – happening or existing one after another without a break

target-setting review **n.** – a meeting to set goals for a business or individual.

think ahead **v.** – to make plans about the future, so that you will be prepared

thrive **v.** – to do well and be successful

time frame **n.** – the period of time in which something is planned to happen

trading hours **n.** – the hours during which business is open

trust **v.** – to believe that someone will do something well and in the way you want

undermine **v.** – to make something less strong or successful

undertake **v.** – to do something

viable **adj.** – If a plan, suggestion, etc. is viable, it is practical and could be successful.

vision **n.** – another word for eyesight; also being able to see or express an idea or goal clearly

Unit 8

acting **n.** – the activity or profession of performing in plays or films

artefact **n.** – an object that is made by a human being, especially one that is historically or culturally interesting

ballet **n.** – a type of very skilled and artistic dancing with carefully planned movements

ballroom dancing **n.** – a type of dancing in which two people dance together using fixed sequences of steps and movements

beverage **n.** – any drink, usually other than water

case in point **n.** – a specific, appropriate or relevant instance or example

certificate **n.** – an official document stating that particular facts are true or that requirements have been met

character **n.** – The characters in a film, book or play are the people that it is about.

classic **adj.** – refers to something of a very high quality that has become a standard against which similar things are judged

collaborate **v.** – When one person or group collaborates with another, they work together.

deconstruct **n.** – to take something apart or analyse it

Department of Education **n.** – the section of government that is responsible for education

display **v.** – to put something in a particular place so that people can see it easily

drawing **n.** – the art of making pictures with a pencil or pen

eco-tourism **n.** – tourist travel intended to promote ecological awareness and done in a manner that limits damage to the environment of the area

engage **v.** – If you engage with something, you get involved with it and feel that you are connected with it.

enhance **v.** – improve something's value or quality

essay **n.** – a short piece of formal writing on one particular subject, written by a student, or by a writer for publication

facilitate **v.** – to make an action or process easier or more likely to happen

foundational **adj.** – forming the base on which something else is built

fundamental **adj.** – very important or essential to other things

heritage **n.** – A country's heritage is all the qualities, traditions or parts of life there that have continued over many years.

host **v.** – If someone or an organization hosts a party or event, they have invited the guests and provided the food and activities

interior design **n.** – the art or profession of designing the decoration for the inside of a house

jewellery **n.** – attractive objects that people wear – for example, rings, bracelets and necklaces – often made with gold and precious stones

monitor **v.** – If you monitor something, you regularly check its development or progress, and sometimes comment on it.

non-fiction **n.** – writing that gives information or describes real events, rather than telling a story

painting **n.** – the art or process of applying paints to a surface such as a canvas to make a picture or artistic composition

photography **n.** – the skills of producing photographs

playwriting **n.** – the writing of plays

poetry **n.** – a form of literature in which poems are created

premises **n.** – the premises of a business or an institution are all the buildings and land that it occupies

preserve **v.** – If you preserve something, you take action to save it or protect it from damage or from getting worse over time

printmaking **n.** – an artistic technique that consists of making a series of pictures from an original, or from a specially prepared surface

raise **v.** – If something raises an emotion or question, it makes people feel the emotion or consider the question

reconstruct **n.** – to form or build something again and try to get an understanding of it

retail **n.** – goods that are sold directly to the public in shops

sculpture **n.** – the art of creating a work of art by carving stone, wood, clay or other materials

social circle **n.** – a group of people who are socially connected; a network of people who interact

stage design **n.** – the planning and making of the area where actors or other entertainers perform

sustainable **adj.** – capable of being maintained or used at a steady level without any problems or causing damage

theatre studies **n.** – the study of entertainment that involves the performance of plays

viable **adj.** – capable of becoming useful or real, of being achieved

Unit 9

ably **adv.** – in a competent or skilful way

amplify **v.** – to make louder

beech **n.** – a type of tree

campaign **v.** – to try to achieve a social, political or commercial goal by persuading people or a government to do something

cast **n.** – all the actors in a play, film, etc.

concept **n.** – another word for an idea

food bank **n.** – a place where spare or donated food is distributed to those who need it

foster **v.** – to look after something and to help it grow

fundraising **n.** – activities to raise money for a good purpose, charity, etc.

humanitarian agency **n.** – an organization devoted to helping people in need, especially in times of war or natural disaster

improvement **n.** – work done on something to make it better

label **v.** – to fasten a piece of paper to something, which gives information about the thing

loyal **adj.** – willing to support someone even in difficult times

nonprofit **adj./n.** – an organization that does not make money from its work

political party **n.** – an organization that has or wants to have political power

prison **n.** – a building where criminals are kept as a punishment

punishment **n.** – a penalty or sanction given for any crime or offence

strength in numbers – the fact that a group of people has more power than one person

take place **v.** – to happen

tight-knit **adj.** – well organized and closely linked together

unpaid **adj.** – Unpaid work is work that you do not get paid for

volunteer **n.** – a person who works without receiving any payment

Unit 10

aqueduct **n.** – an ancient construction used to transport water above ground

Bronze Age **n.** – a period of ancient history from around 3500 to 1500 BC

colonial **adj.** – relating to the management of an empire's colonies

decade **n.** – a period of ten years

geometrical **adj.** – patterns or shapes consisting of regular shapes or lines

go back to **v.** – If something goes back to a particular time in history, it started to exist at that time.

gothic **adj.** – a style of architecture typically from the Middle Ages

infrastructure **n.** – the basic facilities of a country, such as transport, power systems, buildings etc.

label **v.** – to fasten a piece of paper to something, which gives information about the thing

lack of **n.** – a situation in which there is not enough of something

medieval **adj.** – of, relating to, or in the style of the Middle Ages

overlap **v.** – If two styles, periods, etc. overlap, they have some of the same features, times, etc. as each other.

peace treaty **n.** – an agreement marking the end of a war

reign **n.** – the time when a particular king or queen is the ruler of a country

revival **n.** – a time when something becomes popular again

span **v.** – If something spans a long period of time, it relates to that whole period of time.

visitor attraction **n.** – a place that tourists like to visit

Unit 11

assessment **n.** – a consideration of someone or something and a judgement about them

assume **v.** – to think, sometimes wrongly, that something is true

charge with a crime **v.** – to formally accuse someone of committing a crime *cigarette butt* **n.** – the part of a cigarette that is left when you have finished smoking

commit murder **v.** – to kill someone deliberately

convict **v.** – to prove that someone is guilty of an offence or crime

crime scene **n.** – the place where a crime happened

date back to **phrasal v.** – to be made or begun at a particular time in the past

deal with **v.** – to take action on

debate **n.** – a discussion between people who have different opinions about something

deteriorate **v.** – to become worse in quality

determine **v.** – to settle or decide an argument, question, etc. conclusively

displace **v.** – to make something move from its usual place to another place

distorted **adj.** – changed, reported or represented in an untrue way

evidence **n.** – facts or physical signs on which to base proof or to establish the truth

eyewitness **n.** – a person present at an event who can describe what happened

false sense of security – the mistaken feeling that you are safe

fibre **n.** – a long thin thread from a fabric

fingerprint **n.** – the distinctive mark you leave when you touch something with your finger

footage **n.** – film taken with a camera of a particular event

forensic **adj.** – relating to, used in, or connected with a court of law

fragile **adj.** – able to be broken easily

injury **n.** – physical damage or hurt

in place – working or able to be used

intended **adj.** – planned

lawyer **n.** – someone whose job is to advise people about the law and represent them in court

lighting **n.** – lights, street lamps, etc.

naked eye **n.** – If you see something with your naked eye, you do not use a telescope or microscope, etc.

number plate **n.** – the sign on the front and back of all vehicles, that has numbers and letters on it

reveal **v.** – to show something

scale **n.** – a sequence of marks at regular intervals, used as a reference in making measurements

seal **v.** – to close something up so that air cannot get into it

shoplifting **n.** – the act of stealing things from a shop by hiding them in a bag or in clothes

sketch **n.** – a drawing that you do quickly

solve a crime **v.** – to find out who committed a crime and what happened

sophisticated **adj.** – more advanced and using new and clever ideas

suspect **n.** – a person who police think may have committed a crime

systematic **adj.** – done using a fixed plan so that nothing is missed

terrorist **n.** – a person who uses violence, for example bombing a place, for political reasons

thorough **adj.** – done completely and carefully

Unit 12

ambassador **n.** – an important official who represents a country

be made redundant **v.** – If you are made redundant, you lose your job because your employer does not need you anymore.

break the speed limit **v.** – to drive faster than the law says you can

emissions **n.** – the gases given off into the atmosphere *fortress* **n.** – a strong well-protected building

freeway (Am.) **n.** – a major road that can be used without paying a toll (Br. = motorway)

gem **n.** – a precious or semiprecious stone used in jewellery as a decoration

goodwill **n.** – a feeling of wanting to help someone

literally **adv.** – exactly

livestock **n.** – farm animals

millennia **n.** – plural form of 'millennium': a period of one thousand years

pavement (Br.) **n.** – the path for people to walk on next to a road (Am. = sidewalk)

petrol (Br.) **n.** – fuel for a car, etc. (Am. = gas)

raw materials **n.** – materials in their natural state, used for a particular manufacturing process

region **n.** – an area considered as a unit for geographical, functional, social or cultural reasons

rely on **v.** – to depend on something

roadworks **n.** – repairs that are being done to road, especially when this delays traffic

rural **adj.** – relating to the countryside

scholar **n.** – someone who studies an academic subject and knows a lot about it

silk **n.** – a smooth, fine cloth made from fibre produced by a silkworm

tram **n.** – a vehicle that runs on rails on a road, and is powered by electricity from an overhead wire

undertake **v.** – to do something

well worth – If something is well worth doing, there are good reasons to do it.

worrying trend **n.** – a gradual change or development that causes concern or worry

Practice test

blur **v.** – to become less distinct, less clear

brisk **adj.** – lively and quick

clone **v.** – to produce something that is the same or nearly the same as something else

congestion **n.** – the state when there is so much traffic that vehicles cannot move

hub **n.** – the focal point, the centre

pop-up **adj.** – a pop-up shop is set up quickly and intended to be temporary

resilient **adj.** – recovering easily and quickly from problems, shock, hardship, etc.

solitary **adj.** – experienced or done alone

supply chain **n.** – a channel of distribution from the maker of materials or components, to the manufacturer, distributor and retailer, and finally to the consumer

vacant **adj.** – empty